Mastering Influence- Dark Secrets of Persuasion and Mind Control

Mastering Influence -Dark Secrets of Persuasion and Mind Control

I J Nayak

India
2023

CONTENTS

Language and thought are inextricably linked. Plato, an ancient Greek philosopher suggested that we only experience reality through language; Wilhelm von Humboldt considered language the basis of thought; these ideas were formalized into the Sapir-Whorf hypothesis which asserts that a language's structure influences how speakers think; a clear example is how the number of words available for distinguishing colors influences how speakers perceive colors - this concept that limited words limit and channel cognitive choices is something influential manipulators use to their advantage while leading them down this path of thought is crucial and widely adopted over time by philosophers like Humboldt as well.

George Orwell's Nineteen Eighty-Four was an influential book that highlighted fascist governing bodies that use rhetorical strategies as part of their rule, operating with manipulative force on par with any self-centered narcissist or dispassionate sociopath. This book continues to be taught in American schools and one of its greatest impacts was to reveal how language manipulation occurs; specifically by introducing Newspeak as the government language of choice. Newspeak allows the powers that be to alter basic concepts and our perception of reality by restricting language usage. People using it only perceive certain matters while neglecting or not processing all that might be considered inappropriate. Simply stated, Newspeak defines reality for its citizens by restricting language. As an extension, individuality becomes nearly impossible when language restricts speech options for self-expression - adjectives for example are simplified into unfavorable adjectives which prevent individuals from expressing nuanced thoughts about anything outside their scope of understanding and prevent nuanced thought being expressed freely. This allows the government to reframe reality as perceived by their subjects through narrow definitions that limit choices available for self-expression - similar to how political parties often restrict speech options limiting options which reframe reality for all involved.
They use words to create polarized thinking and add layers of interpretation within words themselves, such as calling sexual encounters "sexcrime." On the flipside of that coin are forced labor camps named "joy camps," suggesting positive qualities to what should otherwise be a negative experience - all designed to ensure obedience. This tactic also extends to government branches named for such purposes: The Ministry of Love enforces laws and levies punishments while the Ministry of Peace wages war while The Ministry of Truth acts as propaganda arm for their respective branches - giving them credibility within its ranks.

There are plenty of examples of government officials using reframing strategies to their advantage. During the 2016 US Presidential election, candidate Donald Trump made headlines when he redefined "fake news", an appellation typically applied to sites spreading false stories over social media, to refer to actual mainstream news sources instead. Rebranding actual news sources as fake news certainly had newspeak connotations. When political actors use catch-phrases or catch-phrases that glorify their side or denigrate another, their rhetorical manipulation attempts are employing propaganda techniques in an attempt to limit cognitive choices within their audience and attempt to limit cognitive choices made available by their audience members.

What can these tools be used for in a relationship or workplace setting? We have already seen examples, in our God, Devil, and Charisma series. Rhetorical choices may reveal an answer that remains unsaid.

Sociopaths, psychopaths, narcissists and similar deviant personality types employ many linguistic tactics to gain the upper hand in any negotiation they engage in with their victims. They will attempt to confuse, disorient or otherwise frustrate their targets in order to exert control over them - one tactic used is language manipulation - so it might be worthwhile reviewing some of these manipulative personalities' typical word choices and rhetorical framings from our discussion earlier; we'll also focus on how these tactics may play out in real situations involving victims as we talk through possible resolution strategies when encountering someone similar who uses language manipulation against another victim - we'll focus on discussing what this might look like; we will generally discuss how effective these tactics might work against us all parties involved;
Communication techniques often used in interpersonal relations can cross over into business situations as well.

Start here to understand some of the key phrases employed by sociopaths - those with emotionally detached personalities capable of dispassionately pursuing self-interest to the detriment of others, often accusing their opponents of overreacting - when discussing situations with them. Sociopaths and psychopaths alike often use phrases such as this to shift focus away from any problem or situation and put the burden on to the victim themselves, leading them to think that whatever was bothersome wasn't really so big of an issue in the first place. Sociopaths frequently employ this tactic as an effective means to end conversations quickly and invalidate feelings of their targets. An alternative form of invalidation involves telling the victim they're being ridiculous; another form of rejection with more implied judgment. Not only are you wrong or overreacting; you are also acting illogically - lots can be said with just a few words!

Psychopaths employ similar tactics, with slight modifications. Psychopaths might accuse you of "overanalyzing", an effective strategy used to destabilize situations quickly. Psychotics will often attempt to confuse their targets by suggesting they may be going insane or off their rocker. When you respond to these attempts, they'll simply shut it down with an accusation of over-analysis - all designed to make you question whether your assumptions were indeed right about everything. Psychotics may withdraw, accusing you of creating "drama." Again, this tactic serves to turn the tables. Even when your feelings of injustice are justified, they'll reframe them as something out of line with reality and try to discredit it as part of the argument. Psychotics are experts at gaslighting - an increasingly prevalent technique. Both previous techniques touch upon this issue; but with full-on gaslighting the psychopath will claim they never said what you know they said; given that psychopaths are capable of complex behaviors they could even pull this one off more successfully than any of us would like!

Subtly deceiving themselves and others into believing their false statements is often enough to send shockwaves through victims, prompting them to doubt their own senses and perhaps even their sanity.

Narcissists will use phrases such as, "I've never felt this before" to exaggerate connections between themselves and their victims, yet at the same time use this to establish future control and codependent attention from them. This tactic not only makes their victim feel good about himself or herself, but it's merely a step toward further control and codependency in future relationships. Narcissists often project their weaknesses onto those closest to them and use this tactic when things don't go their way - in this instance it may mean accusing their partner of being paranoid or controlling. When things don't go as planned they use such accusations against their partner as leverage against them - an example of projection. Narcissists tend to be controlling and paranoid themselves; by projecting these qualities onto others, they may make themselves feel better while destabilizing the partner. Another tactic may be suggesting that this manipulator has never experienced this issue with anyone else; this helps reframe so that only you are responsible.

In each of the examples presented above, rhetorical reframing may also incorporate language that serves to push your argument in one direction or another - words such as ridiculous, paranoiac and drama can carry more weight than you realize. Intellectually you may know it to be false, yet being accused of creating drama when in actuality you feel upset is hard to combat. Extending these techniques to other scenarios should prove effective. At work, any coworker or manager with legitimate complaints against an employee with one of these personality deviancies could easily find their complaints reframed as being paranoiac or micromanaging, or that "I've been doing this job for years without hearing these complaints before", thus intimating that their complaints themselves may be the problem.

These are typical examples of how sociopaths, psychopaths and narcissists use language to manipulate. Although individual words may differ depending on who's talking.

Under any given situation, these examples reveal how powerful individuals use language-based strategies to gain leverage in various situations.

Communication Is A Tool

Like any tool, communication can be used for different purposes. A hammer has one main use - driving nails into walls; its claw end serves an additional function - pulling out nails. These two functions of tools work hand in hand, with construction projects often being the main purpose for which they were intended. A hammer may also be used destructively - breaking windows or being wielded against someone's head as weapons are all possible options - although not what was originally intended, but its function has simply changed depending on who uses it.

Some may ask when communication crosses into manipulation as though communication existed on an spectrum. That's simply not how communication works! Communication doesn't switch into manipulation automatically when one goes too far in one direction - rather, communication serves as a tool that attempts to influence. Every effective communication, particularly formal dialogues, relies upon rhetorical tools. No matter how many or which ones you employ to meet the communications goals set for yourself, their use will not put you on a path toward being seen as manipulators. Effective communication towards positive or altruistic ends is precisely that: effective. The Greeks understood this, seeing effective argument as an indicator of truth. If a salesman or doctor respects your wishes and acts with them in mind, their arguments won't amount to manipulation. Even if they convince you to undergo lifesaving surgery despite your fears about surgery, as long as their arguments for it were offered honestly.

So if manipulation doesn't depend on degrees, when does communication cross over into manipulation? The answer lies within motivation - likened to using a hammer as an example: once used with any other intention in mind it becomes an offensive tool or weapon. Communication works similarly. Manipulation does not occur at some threshold of techniques utilized or effectiveness of their use; rather, manipulation occurs when it is employed unfairly to deceive or further an agenda that compromises its target of communication. Just as communication can be both effective and ineffective, so can manipulation. Some individuals are simply ineffective at it, while certain audiences have become adept at recognizing it. If someone approaches you on the street attempting to manipulate, and they fail to convince you otherwise, simply avoid them by walking away; does that mean they weren't trying? No! What the con man was engaging in wasn't straightforward communication or honest persuasion - rather he attempted to manipulate but failed miserably. Sometimes using identical techniques for persuasion or manipulation requires only changing one variable: motive of speaker. In other instances, techniques themselves may be inherently manipulative; such as those we discussed in the last section. Any form of deceit or manipulation is inherently manipulative. Even if your intentions were good, even with fair and effective tactics you would still be engaging in manipulation on some level. Sometimes you might actually have some form of positive outcome in mind; however, your willingness to lie reveals an ulterior motive. A willingness to mislead is, itself, an ulterior motive. This can become complex, so let's keep this straightforward: when your motive for outcome and tactics are positive and fair, we can classify your communication as persuasion. Any time that your desire is to harm or advance yourself above that of your target, mislead or play unfair with communications in any way, or play unfair with communications it reaches a threshold to be defined as manipulation.

Before discussing how dark psychology works and its methods against you, it's essential that we first understand exactly what this form of psychology entails. Psychology, or understanding how the human mind functions, plays an essential part of daily life - from advertising and finance, crime and religion, even hatred to love; thus demonstrating why understanding its principles holds such power over human influence.

Psychology can be an arduous undertaking, which explains why most people lack this skill. Learning all the different principles is not necessary - simply start from these lessons for a solid base to build upon. Reading people accurately, understanding what makes them tick and their reactions in unexpected ways is key. Even then, taking classes and reading countless books might be necessary in order to gain a complete understanding - depending on how far your understanding extends.

So why is understanding psychology and human psychology so essential? Because those who know more can use that power against you.

How is Dark Psychology Used Today?

While some may use dark psychology tactics with the intention of harming their victim, others can use these strategies without manipulating anyone in any negative way. Some of these strategies were first popularised during World War I. Unknowingly or intentionally, our toolbox has expanded through various means such as:

* As a child, you likely observed how adults behaved, particularly those close to you.

* As a teenager, your mind was expanded in terms of understanding behaviors around you.

* You were able to observe others utilizing and then successfully applying specific tactics.

* At first, your use of tactics might have been accidental; but as soon as they began working to achieve your desired goals, they would become part of your intentional strategy.

* Politicians, public speakers and salespeople may have been trained in these tactics in order to achieve their desired goals.

Dark Psychology Tactics That Are Employed Daily

* Love Flooding: Love flooding refers to any form of coaxing people into complying with a request that you want. For instance, if you need someone's help moving some items into your home, love flooding could make them feel good about helping - increasing the odds that they will comply. Dark manipulators might use love flooding in this way in order to make them feel attached or take actions they wouldn't normally.

* Lying: Lying can refer to providing your victim with false or embellished versions of events in an effort to get what you desire done. Lieing may involve telling only part of the truth or making exaggerated claims in order to achieve desired results.

* Love Denial: A form of manipulation which can leave their victim feeling lost and abandoned by their manipulator, is withholding affection or love until you can gain the desired outcomes from them.

* Withdrawal: When this occurs, the victim receives either the silent treatment or is avoided until they meet the needs of another person.

* Limiting choices: A manipulator may grant their victim access to some choices in order to distract them from making those that they do not want them to make.

* Semantic Manipulation: In this tactic, a manipulator uses words with commonly understood definitions to confuse their victim during conversation and then later reveal they meant something different when they used that word; often this alters its entire definition and may cause their desired conversation to progress even though their victim may have been tricked.

* Reverse Psychology: Reverse psychology occurs when you manipulate someone into performing one action only to have them act the other way, knowing full well it was what was wanted by the manipulator all along.

Who Will Intentionally Employ Dark Tactics?

Many different people can utilize dark psychology tactics against you, which could include tactics like those found here. As these people may attempt to use these dark tactics against you, it is crucial that you learn how to recognize their approaches and stay away from them. Potential sources include:

Narcissists: Individuals who possess an exaggerated sense of their own worth often want others to believe they are superior as well. In order to satisfy this desire, they may use persuasion and dark psychology techniques in order to attain what they see as worshipful admiration from everyone they come in contact with.
* Sociopaths: Sociopaths have an impressive arsenal of charming, intelligent, and persuasive traits; yet only act this way when necessary to get what they want. Associativism means they lack any emotions to feel any guilt for using dark psychology techniques for personal gain - including creating superficial relationships as needed to do so.

* Politicians: Politicians can utilize dark psychology to influence voters to support them by convincing them that their point of view is the correct one.

* Salespeople: Not all salespeople use underhanded tactics against you; however, those devoted to hitting their sales numbers could use dark persuasion in order to manipulate people and increase profits.

* Leaders: Dark psychology techniques have long been employed by leaders in order to manipulate team members, subordinates and citizens into complying with their will.

* Selfish people: Selfish people can be defined as any individual who prioritizes their own needs before the needs of anyone else, without regard for whether that will impact those around them in any way. They won't worry about giving others credit where credit is due so that they themselves may benefit; as long as this situation works in their favor it won't matter who loses out, but if someone ends up being affected negatively then that would likely be them instead of someone else.

This list serves two important functions. First, it will help raise your awareness of those who may attempt to manipulate you into doing things you don't want to do, while it can assist with self-realization by keeping an eye out for people looking to gain something out of you.
One of the key goals of this book is to equip you against dark psychology and help protect yourself.

Mental manipulation is a term often heard on social media and mainstream communications platforms, often in relation to large public events, political campaigns or advertising strategies. Most individuals understand what "mental manipulation" refers to but may lack a thorough knowledge of its definition and scope.

Mental manipulation involves shaping and manipulating another person's thoughts to influence them into doing what you want them to. A manipulator influences others through deceitful or unethical means.

Manipulation generally implies some degree of force upon its targets; that is, manipulators will attempt to coerce their targets into doing what they wish despite opposition from targets themselves.

Now, when I talk about brainwashing people like in movies, I don't mean using kidnap and brainwash techniques as is often depicted. What I am discussing are subtle techniques and strategies used to convince others of one thing without their being aware that they're being controlled.

Actually, master manipulators make it appear as though people are acting on their own rather than due to external provocation. Still, there is some force involved with manipulation - for instance television stations force you to watch their programming and advertising in order to encourage you to purchase products or services of sponsors.

However, in this instance, coercion can easily be avoided:

Simply switch channels. However, programming and advertising is designed so you won't want to.

Other forms of manipulation can be much more direct. Political parties and candidates often promote themselves with calls-to-action such as, "vote for the best candidate" and "vote for so-and-so if you value their future". Such overt attempts at persuasion are seen frequently on political campaign ads.

That is why the first part of this book focuses on understanding and recognizing common forms of manipulation. I don't refer to some sort of secret cabal trying to control human minds all over the planet; rather, trained individuals may attempt to influence your opinions to get you behind their agenda.

Once you understand their techniques, not only can you protect yourself and your loved ones from outside influences, but you may be able to promote your agenda successfully. While I am not encouraging anyone to go out there and influence people they come into contact with directly using these techniques; rather use these tactics when necessary to give yourself the edge you need in life.

Relax; we are about to embark on an extraordinary adventure. So just sit back and take the journey.

Though many individuals use dark psychology tactics with malicious intent, you may also use them without harming anyone else. Some of these techniques were either unknowingly or intentionally added to our toolbox due to various circumstances that include:

As a child, you would observe the behavior of adults around you and how they interacted.

* As a teenager, your mind and capacity to comprehend behaviors around you were sharpened considerably.

* You were able to observe others use and successfully implement specific tactics.

* At first, using certain tactics might have been unintentional. But once they proved their worth in getting what you desired, they may become intentional tools of your trade.

* Politicians, public speakers, or salespeople often learn techniques like these in order to achieve their desired goals.

Dark Psychology Tactics That Can Be Employed on an Regular Basis

* Love Flooding: Love flooding involves using flattery to persuade others to comply with your request. For example, if you want someone else to help move items into your home, using love flooding could increase their likelihood of doing so and make your job easier. A dark manipulator might use love flooding in this manner in order to gain leverage against their target.
Make them feel close, then coax them to do things they might otherwise refrain from doing.

* Lying: To lie is to provide someone else with false or embellished information in order to accomplish what you want done, such as telling a partial truth or exaggerations with the aim of getting what they wanted done done.

* Love Denial: Love denial can be devastating for its victims as it makes them feel abandoned by the manipulator. Essentially, this involves withholding affection and love until you've achieved what you desired with them.

* Withdrawal: When this tactic is applied to someone, they may receive the silent treatment or are avoided until their needs have been fulfilled by others.

* Restricting Choices: Manipulators may provide their victim with some choices in order to distract them from making ones they do not approve of.

* Semantic Manipulation: This tactic utilizes words which have widely accepted definitions between parties to the conversation; then later inform the victim they meant something different when using said word in conversation. Changing its definition often shifts the dialogue in ways the manipulator intends despite deceiving someone into giving in to his or her will.

* Reverse Psychology: When someone is told to act in one manner, with the expectation that they will actually respond differently, only for it all to turn out differently than intended by the manipulator. In essence, reverse psychology works exactly how its name implies: to make people behave in ways the manipulator wants.

Who Is Going to Employ Shadow Tactics Deliberately?

There may be many people out there using blackmail against you and can crop up in various aspects of your life, making their presence extremely dangerous.
Learning how to avoid dark psychology tactics is imperative, and some examples of individuals using such strategies include:

*Narcissists: These individuals often possess inflated views of themselves and have the need to convince others of this reality. In order to satisfy their desire to be worshipped and revered by everyone they meet, these narcissists resort to persuasion and dark psychology techniques to reach this end goal.

* Sociopaths: Sociopaths have an air of charm, intelligence and persuasion - but only to get what they want. As they lack any emotions or remorse for what they do, using dark psychology techniques - including superficial relationships - to achieve what they desire is not an issue for them.

* Politicians: Utilizing dark psychology, politicians could convince voters to vote for them by convincing them of the superiority of their point of view.

* Salespeople: Not all salespeople use underhanded tactics against you, but those focused on hitting their sales numbers could use persuasion techniques in order to manipulate others and get results faster.

* Leaders: Dark psychology techniques have long been employed by leaders in order to influence team members, subordinates and citizens into doing what they desire.

* Selfish People: Selfish individuals include anyone who puts their own needs ahead of those of others. These people typically aren't bothered by who benefits in any situation as long as it primarily benefits themselves - if that means others get less, that is fine - but any time one party loses out, it will likely be them not the other one. This list serves two functions. First, it will help make you more aware of those who attempt to manipulate you into doing things that you don't want to do; secondly, it can assist with self-realization. One main goal of this book is for you to recognize those seeking something from you without considering any negative repercussions; that way you can protect yourself against dark psychology.

Who Controls Our Lives It is interesting to observe the long history of manipulation within society. Knowing more about persuasion will allow you to be better equipped in dealing with it.

This chapter will give us a brief glimpse of manipulation as it applies to life and commerce. By understanding where manipulation may exist and who attempts to manipulate you, we will gain an idea of its prevalence in our daily lives and identify those who attempt to manipulate us. Not everyone who manipulates is necessarily malicious - sometimes people may act contrary to who they truly are or even without realizing it themselves! Commercial enterprises use persuasion techniques in order to encourage customers into buying their products and services - recognizing such tactics will assist us in handling such tactics with better success!

As individuals, we like to believe we make responsible choices in life. Unfortunately, not always in full control - especially as children influenced by their parents with no direct say over our upbringing. Once we enter the education system, we become even further manipulated. Teachers provide instruction about social norms and expectations of us in society; later as adults we may even become susceptible to manipulation from politicians who hope to win votes for their causes. Many are persuaded to vote for certain parties based on what they promise for the future, even if they do not support all their policies. This gives politicians power over our lives - are we truly in charge or simply being persuaded?
Later in this book, we will examine various manipulative tactics, both covert and overt. First and foremost, you need to recognize when you are being manipulated so you can counteract it; experts have provided their perspectives on this type of behavior among us.
Recognizing the Art of Manipulation

Where should we be wary in our daily lives?

Persuasive Language Its Pictures tell a thousand stories; words have an even stronger influence in inspiring us, sometimes to the point of manipulation. Have you ever been inspired by an orator whose dramatic speech motivates you into action? And words influence us even when lost completely in a great book; words have power that compels us into believing something even when our senses tell us otherwise! Communication can be used effectively as a powerful force when convincing people to do things they otherwise may not.

* Advertisers and salespeople employ language to persuade us that their goods are exactly what we need - such as using words such as:

Affordable; Convenient; Enjoyable; Time Saving and Guaranteed to satisfy.

Note how all these words make us believe they have confidence in their product or service.

Politicians frequently employ language such as:

"We" - to invite you into their world.

Make yourself feel part of our team

These strategies of communication aim to make us feel included and thus important.

Bullies use both words and aggressive behavior to achieve their own personal agendas.

Criminal predators such as psychopaths, sociopaths and narcissists use persuasive language as an avenue for control over another individual. There are six theories on psychological manipulation; 1 cognitive bias theory was examined herein as one potential form.

There are various psychological processes and theories regarding persuasion that have become widely recognized, one being Anthony Greenwald's Cognitive Response Model from 1968 which still proves its worth today in determining factors of persuasion as well as being used extensively within advertising.

Greenwald proposes that what determines the success of persuasion lies not with words but more with feelings; emotions will play a larger role than words in how easily we are persuaded.

Internal thoughts will include both positive and negative aspects, depending on an individual's personality. This is not a learning process but more about whether someone already views a message with favorable or unfavorable cognitions (cognitions).

Persuaders must rely on their expertise in order to address counterarguments effectively, and stop their target from having sufficient time to develop any of them. Furthermore, the persuader should encourage positive arguments to emerge more readily so as to increase its success rate - this increases "persuasion effect".

Persuasion becomes more challenging if the target has been given advance warning of what you intend to say; this allows them to develop counterarguments if your "message" goes against what they currently believe. Research conducted by Richard E. Petty in 1977 proved this point: it showed that students given notice about an event were less likely to be convinced than those without prewarning.
2 Reciprocity
A well-researched theory to help explain our susceptibility to persuasion lies within the Rule of Reciprocity, based on social conventions. If someone does you a favor or does something good for you, you are more likely to feel obliged to reciprocate by returning the favor in some form or fashion.

Subconsciously, Reciprocity may also come into play. Without realizing it, you may agree to perform or favors requested of you by someone because at one time they did something for you and feel obliged; even if their request would normally make you say no.

Companies often rely on this tactic when trying to increase sales. By offering free samples or time-limited trials, businesses hope that customers feel obliged to return the favor and purchase or renew an agreement.

Reciprocity is a well-established psychological process. It is an adaptive behavior which would have increased our chances of survival in the past; by helping others, you increase the chances that one day they'll help you. But reciprocity may have its downsides too: when someone wrongs us, our instinct to exact revenge may drive us as well.

Academic research backs the Rule of Reciprocity strongly. Burger et al (2009) conducted research that demonstrated how participants are more likely to agree to requests when the requester has done them a favor in the past.

Deception is one of the primary tools in any manipulator's toolbox. It involves providing incomplete or misleading information to their victim, in order to unbalance their way of thinking and leave them vulnerable. Manipulation also includes using intentional body language as a persuader and manipulator.
McCornack's theory enumerates four maxims that define truthful statements; any deviation from these will make the message intentionally deceptive. These maxims include:

Quantity
Quantity refers to the "amount" of information presented. Most of us strive to present just enough data so that the recipient fully comprehends our message without too much or too little being provided; too little could cause confusion; too much could overwhelm. A manipulator, however, would play with that quantity by leaving out certain pieces they consider irrelevant if doing so is likely to work against their argument and this practice is known as "lying by omission".

Qualityrefers to the accuracy of information given. Achieving true communication is considered high quality; otherwise, receivers would hear intentional mistruths - or outright lies - intended to gain the manipulator power.

Relation
Here we discuss "relevance" of information to the message. In order to sidestep an awkward question or obscure their own weaknesses, manipulators often alters the subject with misleading topics in order to divert or misdirect attention away from what really needs to be discussed; or overemphasizing something which will give them greater power over listeners.

Manner Manner of communicating a message. An integral component is body language: we read inflections and facial expressions when listening, which can be exaggerated to mislead the presentation of their message, with the goal of emphasizing their agenda.
Lying to manipulate or persuade someone is nothing new; however, its power has only grown more powerful in today's globalized environment. Social media communication platforms do not always involve direct face-to-face contact between two individuals, making it easier for manipulators to misrepresent information or fabricate falsehoods in such forms of correspondence.

Not all manipulation is necessarily negative; sometimes we need help making good decisions for ourselves and this is where Nudge Theory comes in handy; its positive reinforcement system relies on small nudges for change.

Skinner's studies, or behaviorism, illustrate just how helpful this theory can be. By offering rewards as positive reinforcement, behaviorism can entice individuals to act in accordance with what you wish them to.

Nudging can be seen in this example of how customers were given an additional push toward purchasing the second highest priced item - all for the benefit of the restauranteur! Customers were given this extra boost.

The Nudge Theory can be an extremely effective economic strategy. But its application extends well beyond economics to encourage behavioral changes and shape personal choices - even accepted social norms can be altered through this technique.

Nudging was such an effective strategy that the British Government established a Department Behavioral Insights Team in 2010 in order to help develop policies, which was commonly known as the Nudge Unit.

Although employing "nudges" can have some obvious advantages, using psychological manipulation can violate an individual's civil liberties.

5 Social Manipulation Strategies
Psychological manipulation is one form of manipulation frequently employed by politicians or powerful people to advance their own interests. At its worst, psychological manipulation serves as a form of social control - stripping away individuality while forcing the populace into accepting what is given them - though its positive applications include improving health and wellbeing for instance.

Whoever is in power who uses social manipulation may employ distractive techniques to sidetrack important issues. They would argue that their proposals are designed to benefit not just themselves, but your family as a whole and its future; any differences from them would be seen as wrong and selfish - this type of persuasion treats individuals almost like children; its goal is to make everyone believe everything wrong is entirely their responsibility, while the only solution lies within listening to guidance of experts who know better.

Such a political strategy would involve drawing attention to one social problem while covering up others. This tactic aims to cause social unrest and panic among the populace; by creating unease within society, people will begin demanding changes for improvement. So, in an attempt to hide its problems with health care, one department could decrease their budget for crime prevention causing crime statistics to skyrocket and feeding information designed to convince citizens they know best how to solve crime issues. Politicians feed propaganda by spreading their own truths and facts - these may or may not always be accurate; sometimes even exaggerated information like statistics could be misused to achieve desired effects. Social manipulation takes years before its desired results can be realized.

Psychological manipulation is part of social influence, making all of us social puppets to some degree. Most of us employ psychological manipulation without even realizing it!

As expected by society, it is our responsibility to conform and abide by its standards in order to avoid discordant disorder in society.
Consider for a moment what gadget or home improvement product you would most like to purchase: is it something recommended by a friend, neighbor, or featured online that makes you covet it more? Social manipulation works this way too: we can easily be persuaded by others when our guard is down; whether that be seen as good or bad depends entirely upon individual perspective.

As previously discussed, not all social manipulation is bad; in fact it may even have positive outcomes. While the term "manipulation" might evoke images of unscrupulous people bending people to their will, when used properly it can aid society as a whole. One good example of social manipulation would be health specialists encouraging us to eat more fruits and vegetables (the "5 a day campaigns") or stopping smoking campaigns which have resulted in reduced numbers of smokers as well as lower incidence of smoking-related diseases; such tactics constitute effective forms of coercion at its finest!

6 Gaslighting
Gaslighting can be the cruelest form of manipulation. It is an attempt to cast doubt upon a person's sanity and self-esteem by planting seeds of doubt in them - often using repeated lies as bait until eventually you come to believe them as truths.

Gaslighting is an inhumane form of manipulation in which one person causes another person to doubt themselves and lose all confidence in themselves, leading to complete psychological breakdown and subjugation by an adversarial presence. Gaslighters constantly undermine their target by contradicting them or suggesting they always get it wrong, sometimes to the extent of accusing them of telling lies themselves - an action designed to reduce self-worth before becoming completely subsumed under

domineering control from outsiders who take over by becoming oppressors themselves. When that occurs, they become subject to their oppressor's domineering presence - who become subservient before finally succumbing under domineering influence from outside sources. Gaslighters seek power over them in return and ultimately become victims under their domineering master.
Influencer manipulation is a form of mental abuse often seen in abusive personal relationships. An influencer will use various techniques to make their victim doubt themselves - even to the point of questioning their memories by denying past events that happened between them and themselves.

Gaslighting takes time and effort to become fully effective. A manipulator will wear down his/her victim over an extended period, leading to them doubt their own sanity in turn.

Dr. George Simon PhD is a Clinical Psychologist from Texas university. In his studies of people with distressing personalities, particularly psychopaths, his findings led him to conclude that certain types of personality were very adept at manipulation; using lies and aggressive language they managed to place doubt in their victim's minds until eventually, their target lost faith in themselves and believed what the manipulator said, eventually falling under control of him or her.

Psychology Secrets
Most psychological techniques serve both dark and white psychology applications; their utility depends upon the intent of those employing them.

In this chapter, we will look at various psychological techniques used for illicit purposes.
Dark Persuasion
Persuasion is by far the most frequently employed psychological technique, often utilized in White psychology; nearly all of us have utilized persuasion as part of that discipline at some point or another; however, only few have employed persuasion as an effective form of dark psychology manipulation.

Before delving deeper into Dark persuasion, let's first consider its core components.

What is Persuasion? mes Persuasion is the psychological practice of using persuasive arguments in such a way as to motivate, influence or change an individual's attitudes or behavior in order to achieve desired results.

Persuasion Tips Here are several essential persuasion strategies you must master to become successfully persuasive:

Research to gain expert advice

Be a thought leader - to direct other's in their thinking and lead by example.

Be confident, using declarative statements and assertiveness:

Reducing sarcasm as much as possible.

Sound reasonable and monitor reactions in response to subtle responses; actively listen and suggest rather than demand; actively observe; be emotionally intelligent

Persuasion Tactics
Here are several basic yet important persuasion tactics:

Use the name of the person with whom you are engaging.

Connect personally and establish rapport.

Develop relationships and open doors for reciprocity

Use motivating words Be flexible and adaptive - adapt to suit each target individually (no blanket approach). Utilize NLP's mirroring and matching technique.

Use the Bandwagon effect to your advantage

Create some uncertainty among those you are persuading by creating some sense of scarcity for their attention.

Create suspense through deliberate gaps (information gaps).

Apply the "foot in the door" strategy - make a small request which opens up more doors for later larger requests.

Underscoring the value of your proposition to those you're trying to persuade is key when trying to persuade them of its worthiness, since every person subconsciously asks themselves, "what's in it for me?"

mes The Bandwagon Effect
The bandwagon effect can be described as the collective impact that groups of people can have on individual members within that crowd or group of people.

Below are some key characteristics of the bandwagon effect:

Herd mentality - people tend to conform when persuaded that following others will lead to success Social Proof - people tend to follow what appears to be the most popular cause

Decrying negative social proof (such as littering, logging, bad sexual behavior, bingeing and smoking) may actually promote it. For example, criticizing an increase in absenteeism from 15% to 20% should also reinforce positive social proof by noting the majority of employees (80%+) that have not missed work and discussing those few spoilt apples who remain absent as being negligible compared to what should be emphasized and reduced further.

Deception
Deception can be defined as any act that seeks to conceal, misrepresent or advance something that is false in order to cover-up, discredit or promote an opinion with the

intent of convincing another individual to act in accordance with predefined goals or expectations.

Deception involves manipulating appearances to convey an inaccurate representation of reality.

Deception's essence lies in concealment. Common deception techniques include:

Propaganda involves spreading false information as truth or facts, while camouflage disguises true natures of things; an example might be using charity work as cover in order to infiltrate an area.

Pretension refers to taking on an alter ego; for example, pretending innocence when one is guilty, acting sick when you feel perfectly healthy, pretending grief when actually you're celebrating something important, etc.

Mystification - Create an aura of the supernatural by withholding information or acting in ways which appear supernatural, making yourself attractive to those inclined toward beliefs.

Paltering: Conjurers, magicians and actors often employ this tactic in order to draw people's attention away from themselves and towards you, diverting it in your favor in order to meet personal objectives. This tactic also works well when trying to achieve results through public performances such as concerts.

Types of Deception
Deception takes two primary forms.

Lies by commission (dissimulation) - are active forms of deception. A person engaging in lying by commission directly deceives or lies directly by altering material facts deliberately to their benefit.

Simulation or Omission (Lie by Omission) - Simulation lies are indirect forms of deception in which someone engaged in deceit does not directly alter material facts; rather they conceal those which would have changed the decision-making of those being duped.

Dupery
Dupery, like any act of deception, goes further to gain from victims for personal gain. Dupery involves setting traps or baits which entrap victims before exploiting them for personal or nefarious gain.

Indoctrination
Indoctrination refers to the process of inculcating someone with beliefs without giving them an opportunity for independent critical inquiry.

Strategies used for indoctrination:

Rote training - this practice of imprinting information onto people's memories through repeated action such as repeating mantras during prayers or counting mala beads during praying is known as rote training.

People trained to do affirmation-making are instructed to say words which affirm certain statements, thus creating the impression that those statements are true.

Obstruction of Truth and Facts-this tactic seeks to prevent those being indoctrinated from accessing sources of truth or facts, such as books deemed "satanic". Fear psychology techniques may also be employed such as warning them they'll experience nightmares or be visited by vampire spirits if they read such books.

Confession - Each one of us has a past full of sin. There may be things we did that make us regretful; one indoctrination tactic involves forcing people to confess. Once people do confess, their moral authority diminishes before indoctrinators, leading them down a path of submission toward indoctrination.

Isolation - the main goal of isolation is to remove someone from influences which make indoctrination impossible or more difficult, cutting them off from family, society or normal relationships altogether. Thus, victims may become cut off from family, society and normal relationships, leading them to believe anything said by their indoctrinators without receiving another opinion regarding these assertions from trusted third-parties. Isolation also serves as a form of obstruction when truth and facts cannot be assessed objectively from trusted third-party perspectives.

Guilt Imposition - Guilt imposition is similar to forced confession; however, guilt imposition involves instilling a sense of guilt into the mind of the victim by indoctrinators who find ways of discovering any wrongdoing and then use that act against them to inflict guilt upon them. Just like forced confession, this tactic's primary goal is guilt imposition.
Confession may serve to undermine a victim's moral standing and pressure them into psychological submission.

Phobia Imposition - Psychological fear can be instilled through indoctrinators' indoctrination techniques; victims find it increasingly difficult to function outside their domain of influence. Example of Phobia Inducement Insurance companies use fear-inducing tactics on potential clients by exaggerating potential risks that might occur should the potential client opt not to insure the life or property of loved ones, while governments often resort to instilling fear in order to push through their agendas.

Rituals have an indelible mark on one's psychology, which explains why so many traditions, religions, cults, political organizations and civil groups employ rituals as an element of their practices. Rituals may be performed prior to praying or burial services as well as before war begins - these ceremonies increase susceptibility for whatever propositions might be being advanced by indoctrinators.

Induced dependency - Manipulators often employ this tactic in relationships in which they want to gain the upper hand over their victims, for instance imperialist or colonialist entities that perpetuate poverty before pretending to save it from its fate. They may offer conditional aid or grants that contain conditions designed to increase dependency and make victims more prone to exploitation. Since this deliberate impoverishment would not have led to such extreme poverty or resulted in such generous aid and grants, this induces dependency. Marriage partners frequently allow an insecure partner to create conditions which make their partner dependent; an unsecure husband could make her more reliant.
Once his wife loses employment, an insecure husband can more easily control and manipulate his unemployed spouse since he serves as her main source of financial independence. Lacking financial autonomy renders her vulnerable to the dictates of her husband.

Punishment - By creating an incentive system and offering tests/exams as punishments, those who pass their indoctrination program are punished accordingly.

Characteristics of Indoctrination

Unsurprisingly, indoctrination pervades most aspects of our lives - it takes place in homes (by parents and teachers), schools (by teachers), public life (by politicians and governments) etc.

Here are some key attributes of indoctrination tools:

Fear, Dogmatism, Fundamentalism, Cognitive Closure and Perceived Deprivation as Sources of Indoctrination

There can be various covert and overt sources of indoctrination; here are a few commonly overt sources:

Religious Institutions, Schools and educational establishments

Parents' Guide to Media (Mainstream, Alternative Media and Social Networking Sites).

Politicians
Marriage Partners Brainwashing The term 'brainwashing' refers to the process of dislodging one's existing set of old beliefs from their system in favor of new ones that come without being asked or willingly adopted by someone. Brainwashing occurs without consent.

Brainwashing may take many forms; sometimes it is subtle and involuntary while other times violent. One violent example was forced conversion during crusades and jihad. Victims in such instances are aware of what's happening, yet accept it as an effective coping mechanism to avoid greater harm such as death.

Violent brainwashing typically occurs within militant cults or criminal organizations where victims find themselves trapped without an escape route.

Potential victims of violent brainwashing include:

Prisoners (particularly prisoners of war)

Slaves under Captivity
Kidnapped Victims to Slavery for sale by Captors
Illegal aliens Subtle brainwashing often happens without awareness from its victim; here, the perpetrator looks out for susceptible victims who can be more easily persuaded. Furthermore, these vulnerable victims usually find themselves in dire circumstances, giving rise to psychological voids that desire fulfilment.

Below are a few potential victims of unwitting brainwashing:

Are You Living with Unknown Chronic Illness? If yes, please read this.

Minors who have left home to live alone typically reside faraway.

People who have lost their jobs and are suffering emotionally are in deep despair.

Losing loved ones through divorce or death can be devastatingly painful.

Common Steps in Brainwashing

Following are some of the steps brainwashers typically take when they attempt to brainwash their victims:

1. Isolation
2. Attack on Self Esteem Subjugation Subjection
Testing 5 Love Bombing
Brainwashers understand that family or close circle members could quickly identify what is occurring with a victim and thus rescue him or her, so the initial step they take to subvert a victim is isolating him or her from those close to them, such as family or friends.

Cultic leaders, for instance, may instil negative opinions of close family and friends into victims, creating division between themselves and loved ones as a result of brainwashing tactics used against them by such as psychic vampires who drain energy away and make people chronically ill; the victim may succumb to such brainwashing tactics due to illness and desperation - ultimately isolating themselves from someone who could have saved them from brainwashing altogether.

Attack on Self-Esteem A victim suffering from low confidence or suffering from low self-esteem is vulnerable to brainwashing, and so a brainwasher seeks to achieve this state by attacking their self-esteem.

Brainwashers employ various strategies to undermine their victim's sense of self-worth, such as:

Verbal and physical abuse - often utilized in violent brainwashing techniques to dehumanize their victim and undermine his/her sense of worthiness.

Sleep deprivation - Without adequate restful restful, people are more vulnerable to psychological pressure due to reduced awareness. Without full awareness, brainwashing instructions become easier for an exhausted individual seeking just some peace and quiet so they can fall asleep quickly.

Intimidation-Intimidation is one of the many techniques brainwashers use to force someone into submission without their volition, such as by the threat of punishment or punishment itself.

Embarrassment- this strategy can be utilized if a potential victim harbors some unsavory secret they'd rather stay hidden, for instance using various means to obtain nude photographs or induce marital infidelity in such individuals. Once a brainwasher acquires these materials, he/she begins subtly embarrassing the victim without publicly disclosing anything about this material but using generalized terms which indicate immoral behavior on behalf of their target. The victim understands where these cues lead and is therefore determined to prevent their brainwasher from disclosing these embarrassing contents, giving him/her the upper hand needed to brainwash their victim. Example of brainwashing scenarios include forcing victims into performing rituals that undermine their own worth and self-worth, further subjugating them to their brainwasher. Over time, victims may develop Stockholm Syndrome where instead of fighting back, they begin supporting their brainwasher instead.

Protect the Brainwasher (which, subconsciously, means protecting their "secrets")

Brainwashers use scarcity creation such as the rationing of basic necessities and only release them upon an individual performing under their orders, to subjugate victims. Brainwashing seeks to bring victims under total control so that they become completely submissive.

Below are a few tactics used to subjugation:

Extreme Abuse mes Us vs Them
Love bombing Extreme abuseachtig A victim is subject to extreme abuse; often emotional and psychological abuse is employed, with physical abuse only used for violent brainwashing purposes and not subtle brainwashing techniques.

Us vs Them
A victim is forced into choosing between his/her brainwasher and society as a whole. There is no chance for escape for this victim.

Brainwashed subjects introduce victims who still harbor any thoughts of "them", the outside world. Any attempt by victims to consider remaining with "us", the brainwashed subjects, will lead to severe abuse until they make up their minds to join in their brainwashing and abandon "them".

Test, or Assessment,
Testing takes place to ascertain if the victim has made their choice and no longer desires to join "them", while also testing his/her level of obedience.

Under secret control, victims may be released into "them" (the general population) on condition they return on a certain date and secretly monitored to see whether they choose to come back into "us" (brainwashed group).

If the victim does not want to return, then he or she is kidnapped and returned into our fold - and so the vicious cycle starts again.

In case the victim returns willingly, we move onto stage two, known as love bombing.

Most victims find the journey back into society to be too challenging, thus preferring returning back home rather than rebuilding what was lost.

Love Bombing Once tests demonstrate that a victim has been successfully brainwashed, love bombing techniques may be utilized in order to galvanize him or her into joining.

Love bombing may involve praise, promotion in order of subjects, gifts received etc. Dark seduction "Dark seduction" refers to the use of psychological tools designed to use dark manipulation tactics against individuals in order to coax them into relationships that satisfy only one party's self-interest and do not yield tangible returns for either side involved.

An unscrupulous seducer plays on their victim's desires in order to satisfy their own lustful agenda.

Although seduction is often associated with the opposite sexe, it can also involve someone of the same gender and even those who identify as non-sexual.

Dark seduction does not involve sexual acts alone; rather it utilizes sexual stimulation to achieve certain goals.

Sexual stimulation makes victims less logical and rational and therefore more open to manipulation.

Below are a few techniques of dark seduction:

Love Bombing involves sending provocative expressions and platitudes to others as gifts, with or without being explicitly requested to do so.
Dark seduction's primary objective is to appeal to an individual's primitive Id and reduce anti-cathexis; thus encouraging him or her to break away from super-ego and descend down to Id where hedonism exists.

Erotic actions and rewards may be employed against the victim to reinforce this state of Id and remove all evidence of super-ego or anti-cathexis.

More often than not, indoctrination and brainwashing can help dismantle one's super-ego. Hypnotization, however, is used as a powerful technique for this purpose - drawing someone's mind into an open state where they can be persuaded by any suggestion you provide them with.

An individual under hypnosis is similar to someone asleep walking; their awareness becomes singularly focused on walking without taking in signals from outside sources.

While in hypnotic state, an individual cannot consciously draw references from external sources - only from suggestions. Peripheral awareness decreases or disappears altogether as their mind becomes trapped inside an impenetrable bubble impervious to outside signals that would normally penetrate it.

Hypnotic Induction
Hypnotic induction involves giving someone instructions and suggestions designed to induce hypnosis.

Key features of hypnosis:
Concentrated attention focused on one object or idea Isolation from peripheral awareness

Increased Receptivity to Suggestions The main distinction between white and dark hypnosis lies in the intention of the hypnotist: dark hypnosis aims at exploiting its subject for self-serving gains rather than helping them improve themselves through positive suggestions from within hypnosis.

White hypnosis aims to alleviate traumatic or harmful states of consciousness through helping hypnotics snap out from them quickly and successfully. Hypnotherapy is often considered white hypnosis' main form, often referred to as therapeutic hypnosis.

Hypnotherapy
Hypnotherapy is a form of white hypnotic induction used by medical practitioners for therapeutic purposes. The main goal is to help heal from psychological, emotional, and even physical trauma.

Hypnotherapy can be used as an effective method for pain relief by helping a patient to distance himself from the source of his discomfort, thus lessening sensitivity to that pain.

Facts About Hypnosis: Hypnosis Is Voluntary Willful Children Are More Susceptible To Hypnotism THAN Adults

15% of people are susceptible to hypnotism.

10 percent of individuals can only rarely be hypnotized.

People prone to fantasizing are more vulnerable to being drawn into dark hypnotic induction. Additionally, this could have adverse consequences.

There have been many victims of dark hypnotic induction. Common causes include:

Hypnotized so deeply that you willingly hand over possessions to a hypnotist

Are You Being Hypnotized Into Opening the Door Willfully for Robbers?

Are You Being Hypnotized and Following Kidnappers Willingly to their Den? If that is the case for you, being hypnotized so that you follow them into their den will likely lead to kidnap and abuse of some sort.

Understanding manipulation has long been part of life; it shouldn't come as any surprise that persuasion has long been practiced as a skill. Recognizing what its true essence is is essential if you want to effectively deal with its impact.

In this chapter, we will briefly review the psychology of manipulation to better understand where it may exist in our lives and who might try to exploit us. It can also assist with identifying those who attempt to influence us without us realizing it - for instance a boss might encourage their employees into acting out in ways contrary to their normal personality and behavior; learning how commerce uses subtle persuasion techniques will aid you in combatting its pervasive power.

Our society encourages us to see ourselves as independent individuals capable of making rational choices; however, when it comes to life decisions we don't always have full control. Children can often be heavily influenced by their parents and lack any control over the process by which they were raised. Once inside the education system, we become even further manipulated. Teachers teach us all about social norms and expectations in society; later on as adults we are drawn in by politicians looking for votes. Many are persuaded to vote for certain parties by what they promise for the future, even if they do not believe in their policies. This gives politicians power that can affect our lives directly; are we really in control or simply subject to manipulation by those with skillful persuasion techniques?
Later in this book, we will cover how to address various manipulative methods, both overt and covert. First of all, you must learn to recognize when you're being manipulated so you can counteract it; for this purpose we'll also examine what experts say on this type of behavior that exists among us.
Are You Feeling Manipulated?

What kinds of things must we be wary of in our everyday lives?

Persuasive Language Although pictures tell a thousand words, words can be much more effective when used to motivate, encourage and persuade. Just think back on all those times you were inspired by a charismatic orator whose daring speeches inspired and motivated you into action; or when we got lost completely in a great book with words telling a different tale! Language can be an extremely powerful force when used effectively when convincing others of something; communication is an incredible asset when trying to change people's behaviour or making people change their minds on something.
Psychological Manipulation Theories 1 Cognitive

Psychological processes and theories surrounding persuasion are well known; one such theory developed by Anthony Greenwald in 1968 is the Cognitive Response model. Though created over 40 years ago, its principles remain relevant today and used extensively within advertising and other forms of persuasion.

Greenwald suggested that: What really determines the success of persuasion lies not with words but emotions of the recipient, their internal monologue and whether or not they view the message with favorable or unfavorable thoughts (cognitions). This process does not need to involve learning new material but is determined by whether someone already views it in such ways that influence is more or less easy for them.

Persuaders must rely on their skill as persuaders to overcome any counterarguments that arise against their persuasion efforts. They should prevent their target from having sufficient time to craft any counter-arguments of their own and should encourage positive arguments to come to the fore, giving the "persuasion effect" a higher chance of success.

Persuasion becomes more challenging if an intended target has been forewarned of what to expect, allowing time for them to prepare their own arguments against what may seem counter-intuitive to them. Richard E. Petty conducted research that demonstrated the significance of prewarning in 1977: students given notice about certain events were less likely to be convinced than those without prior notification.

Reciprocity
Rule of Reciprocity provides another intriguing explanation for our susceptibility to persuasion: it relies on social conventions - if someone does you a favor or provides something good for you, you are more likely to feel obliged to return the favor in some form or another.

Unconsciously, the Rule of Reciprocity can occur. Without even realizing it, you may agree to do an action or favor for someone because at some point they have done something good for you - even if this request would normally fall outside your realm of competence. Feeling obliged could even have its benefits;

Companies using sales techniques commonly employ this tactic in order to drive more sales. Companies offer free samples or time-limited trials in hopes that customers feel obliged to return the favor by buying their product or continuing the agreement.

Reciprocity is an established psychological process and an adaptive behavior, increasing our chances of survival throughout history. Helping others can increase your chance of getting help in return, but reciprocity may have undesirable side effects; for example if someone harms you then reciprocity could prompt revengeful responses against them.

Academic research lends support to the Rule of Reciprocity. Burger et al (2009) found that participants were more likely to agree to requests made by someone who had done them a favor in the past.

Information Manipulation Step 3

Deception is one of the primary strategies employed by manipulators's. This strategy involves offering limited and confusing information to victims in order to shift their thinking patterns, leaving them more susceptible. Deceit may also involve employing intentional body language in order to persuade and manipulate someone.
McCornack et al. (1992) conducted a study which highlighted various ways in which messages could be falsified to aid manipulation processes. McCornack's theory rests upon four maxims that govern truthful statements; any breach will render that message as intentional deceit. They include:
Quantity Information "quantity" refers to how much is given out. Most of us strive to give out enough data so that the receiver understands our message - neither too little, nor too much can cause confusion. But manipulators may play with that quantity by withholding certain pieces they feel irrelevant to their argument or by withholding information they feel will undermine it - this practice is known as "lying by omission."

Qualityrefers to the accuracy of information delivered. Truthful communication is of High Quality, while when we breach this principle the receiver hears intentional mistruths which give the manipulator power over others.

Relevance Here we refer to "relevance" of information related to our message. In order to deflect an awkward question or sidestep an uncomfortable discussion, manipulators often switch the subject for their own benefit - either to hide weaknesses within themselves, or overemphasizing something which will give them more power over their listener.

Manner of Delivery A presentation is determined by how it is "delivered". Body language plays an integral part in this. As we listen, inflections and facial expressions can give away where a message comes from; manipulators may exaggerate these features to subtly mislead listeners into believing their message emphasizes their agenda instead.

Deliberately manipulating or persuading others through deceit is not a new tactic; however, its usage has become particularly potent in today's society.
Online and social media communication don't always involve face-to-face encounters, making it easier for manipulators to spread mistruths or exaggerate information. Manipulators could thrive using such forms of communication.

4 Nudge Not all manipulation is harmful; sometimes we need help making decisions that will benefit ourselves in the long run. To achieve this goal, the Nudge Theory can be particularly helpful: expanding positive reinforcement by giving gentle pushes in small doses through various "nudges".

Skinner's studies, or Behaviorism, illustrate how useful this theory can be. By offering positive reinforcement in the form of rewards for desired behavior, this theory can nudge people in a desired direction.

One example of "nudging" can be seen here. Although adding high priced items may appear counterproductive, the results actually increased sales for second highest priced item - giving customers a push towards purchasing it - all for the benefit of restauranteurs and their bottom lines.

Richard Thaler is widely considered the "father" of Nudge Theory and was awarded with the Nobel Memorial Prize in Economic Sciences for his significant contribution to behavioral economics. Nudge Theory provides positive reinforcement or "nudges."

The Nudge Theory can be an extremely effective economics theory; however, its application extends far beyond economics to encourage behavioral changes and influence personal choices as well as alter accepted social norms in such ways.

Nudging has proven such a success that in 2010, the British Government established a Department Behavioral Insights Team dedicated to policy development - commonly referred to as the Nudge Unit.
"Nudges" can have obvious advantages for society as a whole, yet using such psychological techniques to influence people may violate individual civil liberties.

5. Social Manipulation
Also referred to as psychological manipulation, social manipulation can be used by politicians and other powerful individuals for personal gain. At its worst form, it serves as a form of social control by taking away individuals' individual rights to force the populace into accepting what has been given them; but social manipulation may be used positively when used for improving personal health or wellbeing issues.

Social manipulatorss employ distractive techniques to divert from important issues. Their proposals would presumably benefit everyone, including your family and its future; any differing opinions would be wrong and selfish - this type of persuasion treats individuals like children; this system tries to convince the crowd that everything that went wrong was their responsibility, so listen carefully when advice from experts comes your way to find resolution.

Such a political strategy would put forward one social issue while concealing another - in order to generate social unrest and panic among the populace and bring changes they demand. One such example could be when one department wants to hide health care problems by decreasing crime prevention budget and thus driving crime statistics up exponentially; information will then be fed back out on crime problem solutions by politicians disseminating their truths and facts which may not always be accurate (ie misuse of statistics).
Social manipulation could take years for its desired result to manifest.

Psychological manipulation is an integral component of social influence. Professor Preston Ni of Communication Studies published an article in Psychology Today outlining this technique where one party recognizes another's weakness before deliberately setting out to cause an imbalance of power in order to exploit victims for personal gain.

Does this make us all social puppets? In part. Most of us comply and conform to expectations in order to avoid anarchy within society.

Think for a second about what product or gadget you would most like to purchase: did a friend suggest it or own one already? More likely it is something someone else already owns or that you saw advertised online, making you want it even more. This is just another form of social manipulation; we can easily be persuaded if we let down our guard; whether that is good or bad is up to each individual to decide.

Social manipulation does not always equate to bad. When used properly, social manipulation can actually benefit society as a whole. For example, health specialists' efforts to convince us to consume more fruit and vegetables through campaigns such as the "5 a Day Campaigns," or even campaigns against smoking which has reduced smoking numbers resulting in lower disease-related risks are examples of successful coercion tactics at their best.

Gaslighting - the cruelest form of manipulation
Principles such as knowing you are being fed false information leads to it eventually being accepted as truth.

Gaslighting is an unethical form of manipulation; gas-lighters cause their victims to doubt themselves and lose all confidence in themselves, ultimately leading them to question themselves further. This leads to immense suffering as their self-worth erodes away. Gaslighting aims to destabilise its target, creating psychological havoc for them. Manipulators will constantly put down their target by contradicting them or convincing them they are always wrong; sometimes leading them down this path until even being accused of making up lies about themself. This is why victims lose all self-confidence; once this occurs, they are completely controlled by a domineering influencer - it is an example of mental abuse commonly found within abusive personal relationships - with constant attempts made at making their victim doubt themselves and question everything they remember saying or doing in past interactions with that influencer. Eventually even memories themselves are called into question by these techniques used against their victim by making them question even what has already been said and done in past interactions with that influencer.

Gaslighting requires time before it becomes fully effective; its perpetrator will gradually wear down their victim, until eventually leading them to doubt their own sanity and question whether a manipulation was taking place.

Dr. George Simon PhD is a Clinical Psychologist from a Texas university who has studied people with problematic personalities. The results of his studies led him to the belief that certain personalities, particularly psychopaths, are adept at manipulation; distorting facts and using aggressive language in order to cast doubt in their victims' minds and cause them to doubt themselves and ultimately believe the manipulator is correct; ultimately becoming vulnerable targets under his or her control.

Gaslighting isn't limited to individuals either; it has also been utilized by political entities. Maureen Dowd is one such author and columnist that uses this tactic. She asserted that Hillary Clinton's administration used gas lighting techniques against an opponent - Newt Gingrich of the opposing political party was frequently goaded into appearing hysterical by these techniques. Journalists and psychologists also believe Donald Trump used such methods both during his presidential campaign and while in office. For example, they note how often he says something before later retracting it or deny even saying it; which they class as classic gas-lighting techniques.
Your partner is deceiving and manipulating you

Let's examine some examples of manipulation that have emerged in personal relationships, perhaps you can recognize some of these characteristics within yourself?

Manipulators tend to be obsessed with control; the more power they possess, the deeper their teeth go into victim.

They will violate other people's personal boundaries through acts such as snooping and spying or taking bold open actions. To enable them to do this, nothing personal such as phones or computers will be allowed into your possession; your passwords may even be stolen without you knowing. Meanwhile, they fiercely guard their own boundaries if their personal space is compromised in some way.

Forceful actions such as blocking you from seeing certain friends may occur when someone refuses to share what belongs solely to them, such as stopping you from visiting your own social circle. At first they will make clear their dislike of these acquaintances while at heart they view them as potential threats; jealousy takes its course and may even turn aggressive.

If you make decisions without consulting them first, they will not be pleased. They don't want you to exercise free will or else it may lead to one day leaving them!

Control can come in the form of advice; however, you don't have much of a choice in accepting it. They are instructing you on what to do and how to act. Manipulative partners tend to want a thorough knowledge of your daily schedule and any deviation from it will likely prompt them to investigate you further. Should anything come up that takes them by surprise, they will certainly question and interrogate about it.

Notice they often criticize whatever you say in public and belittling your opinions and thoughts as a means of asserting their power over you.

Not only are these people quick to criticize you, they often go the extra mile: accusing you of lying or having poor memories; sometimes even having the gall to call you manipulator!

Controlling manipulatorss can never be satisfied; when you think you have reached that goalpost, they move it once more - leaving you uncertain of exactly where your relationship stands.

Are You Engaged in an Abusive Relationship? Without question, manipulators relationships will likely be unhappy ones. Manipulators tend to be unpredictable and may suddenly turn violent when their rules are violated.

Breaking out of an abusive relationship is never easy, but there are resources that can assist. Once it is safe to do so, search online for local organizations that support victims of abusive partners. Also delete your browsing history as nothing will remain private to a manipulator. Stressful at first, but necessary help must be sought out immediately.

Your friends are taking advantage of you to manipulate you into making their moves.

No doubt it can be challenging to form bonds in new environments, and sometimes this process can even feel intimidating or hostile! When this occurs, however, people often feel like fish out of water - these feelings of alienation should never go ignored! We all require friends in life, and learning how to attract them should be seen as an essential skill that all individuals possess. Human beings are social animals by nature and seek companionship from others - there are very few exceptions to that rule!

Selecting Friends - Create an ideal profile of what sort of friends you would like.

Here are three broad categories of friends:

Hello and Farewell to My Acquaintances (Friends).

People you meet through common environments - like work - tend to become your friends almost automatically, such as by saying hello and goodbye when meeting for the day; once outside this shared space however, these friends (which may only really be acquaintances) rarely remain involved beyond these interactions; although it's nice knowing them and taking advantage of their skills whenever necessary they may not necessarily count among your true allies (the Greeks believe you can only count true friendships on one hand - something to keep in mind!).

Drinking buddies, golf partners and shopping companions - fun-time friends come and go in life. They share with you those things which make life fun because they themselves enjoy it, laugh often and take pleasure from spending time in each others company. While such friends don't necessarily engage in long conversations about life's meaning or climate change reality, these loose social connections that form over time become invaluable companions.

Everybody likes having fun, so when the opportunity presents itself, everyone has an enjoyable experience together - though there is little in terms of depth in their relationship with you.

Soul friends

These are your 3:00 am phone call friends - those you can count on being ready and willing to talk if you disturb their sleep at 3 am! With these people by your side on a road trip you won't kill each other before reaching Route 66!

Long, meaningful conversations, shared secrets and mutual support define these friendships. People who stay by your side, through thick and thin, are true soul mates; these individuals understand you intimately while you reciprocate their kindness in kind. Some friends can be there from birth until death, while others you meet along the way. What sets these friendships apart from those that fade over time or average companions is their depth of relationship. Soul friends are hard to come by and when we do meet up again it can feel as though no time has passed at all. You pick up where you left off because you know each other so well; as though fate had preordained that these would be your friends. Soul mates reflect our identities and what's important in our lives; moreover they're there when you need someone because they know exactly who we are.

Forming real friendships takes time.

True friendships don't happen overnight. Over time, lasting and intimate friendships form through genuine chemistry between those involved. Like romantic relationships, true friendships rely on this same fundamental chemical exchange which speaks directly to both parties involved - like an inner song which speaks directly to both. You know when it's real because these bonds don't form themselves - rather, they exist preexisting realities which you recognize and act upon. When true soul friends enter your life for the first time, their impact will be undeniable: you will know immediately that someone with whom you connects instantly is meant for them (along with being)!
Soul Friends can play an invaluable role in your life until its conclusion, whether physical or spiritual. We know they're there, knowing we can pick up the phone and call at any time to find them ready to chat; these friends truly make life worth living! That is what makes them special and incredibly essential.

Though it is easy to recognize our soul friends at first sight, the world can often make this difficult. Yet once formed, soul friends remain persistent despite our culture's distrust: they won't give up looking for you and they won't stop trying; in time the bond between you will become indestructible and you'll have made an ally for life.

Here is how you can become adept at making new acquaintances:

Have You Overthought

Have You ever felt awkward meeting someone, only to quickly feel at ease in their presence after just two minutes of meeting them? Remember that meeting a new person gives no clue as to their character or behaviour; therefore it would be futile for you to overanalyze everything?

And again, presuming meeting new people will be scary only serves to make you fearful in the moment and can turn meeting someone new into something you dislike or dislike altogether. Most often when we feel shy towards people it is due to fear that prevents us from making meaningful relationships that last a lifetime - bad experiences with other people hinder this growth process significantly; therefore it is crucial that we remove ourselves of this illusion of scary meetings as soon as possible! To counter this tendency and ensure we form meaningful bonds we should abandon any presumptions about meeting people will make us fearful, wary or dislike it altogether - disabuse yourself of this notion so you're freed up ready to form meaningful long lasting bonds which should last lifelong. Thusly it would be best if we displacing ourselves of this illusion that meeting someone will make us wary or detestable encounters will happen; usually leading us down this route of feeling awkward or shy towards someone (or any encounter happening). Life has us into individual silos of isolation which makes us suspicious, making life tough and trying to form lasting connections can take decades! The solution herein lies disabusing yourself of this myth that meeting someone is going to make meeting someone or anyone new - instead try disabusing yourself of this notion that meeting someone will mean fearing them outright from meeting the idea that meeting someone new means doing anything at all...
Meeting strangers can be daunting, so stop overthinking about how to approach that first conversation; how to build meaningful connections that could enrich your life. Overthinking these important relationships could result in us remaining lonely and isolated people who never really connect in an authentic or lasting way with one another as humans are meant to do.

Who knows if the other party is nervous about meeting you? In these uncertain times, most of us feel untrusting towards one another and wonder whether anyone we encounter has genuine motives and intentions when we meet them. Most likely they do; trust has been lost between individuals.

Relax and form in your mind a positive image of that first meeting; one which portrays health. Unfortunately, many may judge you unfairly upon first glance. Everybody carries around cultural assumptions about those worth knowing. You likely do too. The key to opening yourself to others and allowing the universe to connect you is opening yourself up and allowing things to unfold organically - this works wonders! Friends worth having are aware that making judgments based solely on superficial characteristics is unwise. Fear resides only within our minds - remove it! Put aside any preconceptions and fears and trust your intuition instead to read people effectively. Trust yourself and your knowledge - you have learned enough about people to recognize when they're being honest or not, by reading their mannerisms, speech patterns and nonverbal indicators that reveal who they really are. Trust yourself and rely on yourself; there is nothing to fear; no need for suspicion or hesitation!

Now you are more than prepared to jump headfirst into social interactions and find like-minded individuals as friends. Your newly gained skills from practicing social psychology should make the search much simpler.
Establish very quickly who is bad and who is good. Although the Big Bad Wolf may still exist, you have become a proficient and capable socially aware individual; no longer vulnerable to being fooled by anyone pulling the wool over your eyes. Your new knowledge makes it simple for you to discern who among those you meet might become your true friends; no more guesswork here - now that you understand the ropes!

Move at Your Own Pace
If you have been out of social contact for an extended period, meeting new people might feel daunting as you start back into it (say at a seminar or party). Take it at Your Own Pace However, you can avoid that dilemma by seeking out friends or acquaintances you know will be present at an upcoming event and meeting up with them prior to attending it - this will put your mind at ease when reentering social situations. By the time you arrive at an event, your anxiety should have subsided significantly. Knowing someone will be present may introduce you to others while your friends will likely sense any tension you are feeling and be there as support - never be reluctant to ask someone you know for assistance; that is what friends are there for! As we've discovered throughout this book - they provide invaluable support!

Are You Seeking to Reestablish a Social Life After Being Isolated? Here Are Some Effective Solutions To Make the Transition Easier:

Start by reaching out to acquaintances - hello-bye bye is an easy first step with minimal risk involved.

Expand your social circle to include small groups of friends you already have; simply to observe how people relate; getting back in the habit of being around people in groups without it feeling intimidating or intimidating. It doesn't need to be intimidating; take things slowly.

Expand your social circle by joining your friends at meetings they are attending with new people. When they hear that you want to lead an active social life again, most will be happy to help!

Step outside your comfort zone and accept invitations to socialize with people outside your usual circle of acquaintances. They say the sweetest fruit lies at the edge, so step out! Enjoy new experiences with new people while learning more about yourself and others alike - why shouldn't people want to meet someone as fascinating and intelligent as yourself?

Be pro-active in socializing! Take an active approach to meeting new people.

Once you are comfortable with resuming social contact and no longer feel isolated from others, you can pro-actively seek out people whom you already know as well as newcomers to you. Friends and acquaintances provide the basis of social connection but you should expand further out into areas that may be unfamiliar such as:

Join a group that shares your hobbies and other interests.

Register to participate in workshops or take courses of study that appeal to you, such as workshops or courses of study that share an interest. It will be easy for you to make friends in such groups where all members share common goals.

Volunteer and you'll find yourself enjoying serving while making new friends in the process. Not only that, but volunteering provides the perfect way to develop skills and aptitudes you may have been hoping to sharpen. Like workshops or groups, sharing an interest provides a common bonding point among volunteer group members - and volunteering is no different!
Accept invitations to birthday parties, social functions and other gatherings where people you want to connect with could meet up. Break through any barriers which might prevent the people you want to meet from coming forward.

Attend social events and "meet ups", with people who share similar interests. Additionally, going out to bars regularly may help; there are people everywhere just looking for someone interesting to talk to; maybe like you they want a way out of isolation or social stagnation too! You are the only one responsible for expanding your horizons - no one else will push them outward for you.

Join online communities - these may be virtual, but I know from personal experience they can lead to real world friendships. For example, I have met many real world friends through Facebook and other online communities; sometimes sharing your thoughts in writing makes communicating easier than verbally; this could help foster lasting connections that last beyond an initial meeting! Plus, you get to analyze potential new friend's writing style before actually meeting them!

Take the Initiative
There's no need to wait around for people to approach you; after all, they may be as reserved as you are. Nobody's born knowing anyone except family; even then, meeting people can often be hit-or-miss. Simply approach people using simple questions like "how are you" and "where are you from". Being open towards those around you will make an incredible difference in how readily people will open up to you!

Remember you are trying to break the ice between yourself and a stranger, so do not over-talk. Be friendly but not intrusive, and don't become frustrated if other don't respond immediately - put yourself in their place whenever possible.
Employ the lessons from this book to evaluate where they stand, and meet them there. Be gentle when making judgments of others - everyone judges everyone else at some point! Take time for engagements between individuals where both participants hope for mutual revelation.

Reject any temptation to become judgmental.

No one is perfect - and that includes you. Human nature leads us to evaluate people quite harshly before getting to know them, which stems from our survival instinct and tells us to avoid those who could potentially cause us danger. But modern people have more effective tools at their disposal, including nonverbal language skills that allow them to identify people who don't match what they want in a companion.

Remaining open to those we encounter is the gateway to deeper friendships, as it helps us be more accepting of others' styles, looks, or attitudes. Not rejecting people because of minor quirks is key in becoming more accepting of who can enter our circle - that's the secret! Sometimes the most unlikely person becomes our truest friend over time. Everyone searches for friendship but should constantly ask themselves if we meet our own criteria before selecting friends to spend their lives with. As I've stated repeatedly throughout this book, knowing yourself is key to knowing others - don't overlook addressing your own challenges before dismissing potential friends due to theirs!

Chapter 6: Understanding The Mechanisim Of Emotional Manipulation

Humans are emotional beings with little regard for logic or rationality, leading them to make decisions more based on emotions than logic and reasoning faculties. That is reflected in media reporting; often portraying or reporting incidences with emotional bias that could provoke similar responses from audiences when broadcasted to them.

An important element in understanding how people respond to persuasiveness lies within emotions. Emotions provide abundant energy that allows us to complete any task at hand; even selling is determined by emotional stimuli generated during presentations; it does not matter how logical you may present things; ultimately the prospect must purchase your product due to his responses triggered during those talks.

On the other hand, logic relies on facts and figures; that is the rationale and reasoning behind any issue at hand. Unfortunately for salespersons who rely solely on logic when selling products and services; if their philosophy hinges more heavily on emotions then sales will come more readily and successfully.

Do you believe humans are rational beings? Based on what logic dictates do decisions and opinions form? Do human react differently depending on facts constantly presented? These are all essential questions for an inquiring person in order to gain an insight into how emotions and logic interact, influencing other humans positively in a positive manner.
Your ability to deliver logical information emotionally will elicit more responses in your audience than simply relaying facts and logic without emotional resonance, which inevitably result in no positive responses from listeners. Reason persuades men while emotion motivates someone into taking decisive action which yields great results.

Let us look at a few ways you can influence others through a combination of emotions and logic, such as:

Establish a Common Identity With Others

One method of controlling people is through building rapport and finding common ground with them as much as possible. A popular idiom states "It takes two people to tangle", so in order to influence someone, both parties involved must share similar goals, experiences, and ideas - this way it becomes much easier. Common grounds in partnerships or relationships tend to be easier when people share similar identities rather than cultures being an added layer. When we create similarities of character we become united through shared goals and objectives, emotional support from one another, logic of shared beliefs shared collective vision mission becomes reality.

Profoundly Exploring Your Partner's Belief System

One cannot have a deep or mutually satisfying relationship with someone they do not fully understand in terms of personality traits and other necessary psychological tendencies. By studying their belief system deeply, however, you can better comprehend them and gradually influence them for your benefit.

Searching for Ways to Acknowlear their Biases

Influencing someone with different beliefs is often difficult, no matter the quality of your logic. Instead, look for effective strategies to appeal to his biases by playing the bias card effectively. How can you do this? By engaging him directly about these matters.
Attracting someone requires finding out their preferred ideas and points and then presenting them. With this approach, your target will feel relaxed around you and more likely give access to his or her private life.

Avoiding Fight or Flight in Your Discussions

Influencing people using logic and emotion works best when meetings and discussions are conducted without instances of fight-or-flight behavior, such as conflicts and misunderstandings in relationships that lead to flights of flight or fight. At such moments, rationality becomes misinterpreted, goals become unmet, and arguments cannot make progress against an atmosphere of fight-or-flight.

An expert manipulator's goal is to form an unhealthy long-term relationship with their target and maintain complete control over them, which will benefit only themselves. An effective partnership requires equal support between its participants. If one partner always seems to offer more, that could be a telltale sign that your spouse may not be being honest about his intentions in your relationship. Psychological manipulation occurs when one party attempts to create an imbalance of power with the aim of taking advantage of another person. Manipulation may manifest in various ways, yet one common thread between all is that one individual, the manipulator, will benefit while another individual - usually known as the victim - cannot be harmed. Some individuals become involved in relationships without realizing they've entered toxic ones. At first glance, their partnership may seem harmless without any indication that later stress and complications await them when dealing with the manipulator. Coercion methods such as this one enable manipulators to reach and take control of their target without knowing them personally. Naturally, relationships would not begin with drama or draining autonomy tactics from a manipulator; when starting off their goal would see them go in another direction altogether; with time this type of approach may become effective as more time passes by.

Initial attention-seeking behaviors will likely not cause them any problems; however, when their goal becomes deeply personal and important to both of them, this could pose some obstacles to progress.
At this point, the manipulator begins altering strategies. This change won't take place overnight but may take several weeks so as to reach their objectives in time. At this stage, their focus may have become so focused around maintaining and strengthening the marriage that any issues or abuse are overlooked more readily than before.

Evidently, there are certain indicators that point towards someone being a manipulator in your relationship. It is wise to check these signals if you suspect anyone in your marriage may be poisonous and causing trouble or potentially being used by outside forces as an influencer or manipulator:

Manipulators will encourage you to step outside of your comfort zone in various ways, with social pressure, physical force and psychological manipulation all used as weapons to divert interests away from what they should be pursuing. They become the one in control and ensure their interests go off track with one another's. They become the one with power over you throughout this journey.

As soon as your confidence begins to decline, manipulation becomes easier for anyone trying to take advantage of you. Our trust is quickly taken back from us as manipulators's quickly take advantage of it by making us feel less-than-great and making use of our weaknesses for personal gain.

Secret Treatment. In this technique, one takes any small slight from their manipulator and magnifies it to create an unpleasant situation for themselves and threaten their goal. We utilize silent treatment by providing email alerts, voice mail notifications, texts messages and emails until finally we end it when necessary. Managing to keep everything under control while knowing when silence treatment has finished can only bring more problems for themselves and everyone involved.

Journey of Remorse. No one likes feeling responsible, so when experiencing guilt we try our hardest to alleviate it as quickly as possible. A manipulator knows this well and will use every excuse they can find to explain his actions away.
Unhealthy marriages often become mired in unresolved conflicts that remain unresolved for various reasons, with no contact occurring between partners and no intention of the manipulator to resolve conflicts intentionally. If that is your situation, it would likely be easier and better if you faked yourself into thinking the dialogue has started or ended instead of working collaboratively together to solve this issue.

Now we can appreciate that this approach to marriage isn't ideal. No one wants to feel trapped in a relationship in which another individual always seems to have control of our lives and makes decisions for us, rather than our lives being managed independently by ourselves. So without taking full advantage of ourselves, we must find someone to support this strategy without us taking advantage of ourselves. However, before moving too quickly forward we must first answer some key questions to determine whether our spouse may indeed be manipulative. As soon as we've gone through this guidebook, you should have a better idea if your friendship is coercive or not. Some measures you can take to protect yourself are acknowledging your rights if one of these partnerships occurs. As friendships can develop over time, it may become challenging to remember how to stand up for yourself when your needs have been ignored by a manipulator. You should never forget that your fundamental rights must always be upheld and should always be respected. There are various freedoms at your disposal, such as respecting others, expressing opinions and desires freely, setting personal goals without being influenced by another and saying no to others. Furthermore, having different opinions than someone can ensure psychological, mental and emotional security and allows for living a fulfilling life independent of another individual if desired.

These privileges may be taken away in the long run from you by manipulators(s). By maintaining checks that provide for effective decision-making and acting upon what they state, these benefits help maintain checks. But before entering any situation again, remember to think ahead. When confronted by one, be observant. Take your own advice seriously when speaking out against an authority figure who wants you to act against their wishes.

Reclaim your freedoms, take a deep breath when talking to a manipulative friend, and try. Only you are the master of your life; so stay away. Staying away is key when dealing with manipulators friends - do whatever it takes to stay clear! Keeping them at arm's length is often best practice. If this is too late, at least try to create some space between you both. Giving them another opportunity to learn about you, assess your vulnerabilities, and devise plans to exploit any future encounters with someone dishonest is only giving them more chances to take advantage of you and exploit your future plans. Staying away from dishonest individuals is the first and only effective defense. When you feel an incentive to change, take the opposite course. Note that manipulators attempt to make you feel bad, in an attempt to help reunite and use you again for their benefit. It would be in your own best interests to stay away from these people; don't fall into their trap by giving into feeling sorry about yourself or supporting their cause.

An additional aspect of manipulators behavior is exploiting your vulnerabilities. Once they know your vulnerabilities, he or she can exploit them fully against you - leaving you feeling inadequate, often punishing yourself over confusion caused by them, making it easy to blame yourself and often punish yourself constantly as punishment from them mounts up. They know this will allow them to maintain control for as long as possible by continually shifting targets so you never reach standards you set - creating inexcusable confusion that allows them to keep achieving their intended destinations.

Do not allow this manipulation to continue. We seek to use you and blame you for whatever shortcomings there may be so you continue feeling bad and seek validation from them in order to feel better. Beware the manipulator's claims that all this blame lies with you alone - none of it is truly your responsibility; all is done simply to make you feel worse.

Making the company and your privileges more likely to give, knowing why and learning to say no will diminish a manipulator's control over you. Knowing why, yes and learning how to say no are fundamental rights we discussed earlier, yet many fail to express them every day. Knowing when it's your time means more control for everyone involved! Knowing when it is your turn requires some learning if you want to avoid becoming part of their manipulation scheme. Knowing why yes means yes but learn to say no if necessary. Partnership manipulators's goal is always saying yes despite information and strategies they use on you if that makes them comfortable saying yes when things do not needing be expressed - understanding this fundamental right should be expanded upon since this fundamental right may go neglected on many fronts when speaking up is not given enough consideration or practiced every day either through manipulation techniques or otherwise failing in communicating it fully on daily bases when needed.

If we fear hurting someone's feelings and worry that their attitude might shift if we refuse assistance for them, saying yes can often leave us crying--it takes great courage to say yes to someone else! Unfortunately, this happens on an almost regular basis. Imagine dealing with a manipulator. Knowing how to assert yourself against them may be challenging at first, but knowing how to effectively speak out against their manipulation will give you power back over your situation. Not everyone will like that decision and you must fight to maintain your independence. Saying 'no' without feeling any regret will allow for a freer and healthier lifestyle overall; being in toxic relationships should never be seen as something positive. Partnering with manipulators involves entering into a relationship reliant on meeting their needs, with potential losses for both parties in time. Unfortunately, being trained into thinking this way makes them unaware they're engaging in such relationships until it's too late. Step one in solving any marital crisis should be learning how to spot signs of deceit, coercion or other difficulties that might be plaguing your relationship. Undergoing marriage takes time and courage, especially as its primary goal has long been to build confidence and self-esteem during difficult times. But when everything does come together successfully and the target finally realizes their dream, the rewards can be substantial.
Learn where you stand and strengthen it; then you may see that life changes without having to use an outside source to do it for them.
Persuasion When people attempt to understand what it means by "persuasion," their answers often vary greatly. While some may turn their thoughts towards advertisements or commercials that encourage consumers to patronize certain products or services over others, others' may turn toward politicians trying to change voters' minds in order to win an extra vote at the polls - both examples serve the purpose of persuasion. Both forms are valid examples as these messages attempt to change people's perception of subjects under discussion.

Dark persuasion differs from normal persuasion in that its motivations do not always benefit those being persuaded; normal persuaders attempt to persuade for the good of those being convinced while dark persuaders often seek gainful motivations that aren't always beneficial to those being persuaded. A dark persuader must gain full knowledge and understanding of whomever they wish to influence in order to identify what motivates them most effectively before engaging in any persuading or persuading behavior from that person before proceeding further with tactics or persuasion tactics if appropriate.

Though persuasion always has moral ramifications, dark persuaders tend not to worry too much about these. While aware of them, their focus remains squarely on reaching their objective(s).

Persuasion is an everyday psychological phenomenon. You could either be the one persuading someone else or being persuaded, with motivation being key. Persuasion plays a large part in mass media, politics, advertising and legal decisions alike - its effectiveness being determined by various methods used for persuasion that influence its subject.
Persuasion stands out as a distinct and essential form of mind control from brainwashing and hypnosis, both requiring subject isolation in order to alter their minds and identities; persuasion does not necessitate isolation as part of its methodology.

To achieve our desired goals, manipulation is employed against individual subjects; persuasion may also be used on one individual; however, large-scale manipulation could potentially alter the beliefs and decisions of entire societies or even communities.

Persuasion may be more effective at changing minds than direct manipulation because it has the ability to sway multiple individuals at once.

Numerous individuals make the mistake of believing they have immunity against persuasion because they believe they will always be able to see through every sales pitch that comes their way and use logic to reach an appropriate conclusion.

People won't always succumb to every argument presented, especially if using logic is used. Additionally, persuasion may not take hold if an argument does not align well with someone's beliefs despite how strong its proponent may appear to be.

But there are people who understand how to use persuasive messages to persuade others to purchase new gadgets or products in the market. Their subtle persuasion will often go undetected by its target, making it hard for them to form opinions about information provided them.

Any time persuasion is mentioned, one tends to associate it with negative associations such as conmen or salespeople trying to convince you that changing your perspective will benefit them and pushes until this change has taken place.

Persuasion can be used both for good and evil; persuasion in sales and conning practices being two examples, with persuasion being used both ways; for example between international bodies or in public service campaigns using persuasion as part of diplomacy agreements and campaigns for good causes being examples of dark persuasion used effectively and for positive effect respectively. It all boils down to how this persuasion process is brought into play.

When seeking to change someone's mind by persuasion, they will require tools and strategies for successful implementation of persuasion techniques in order to succeed.

Each day that passes will present their target with different forms of persuasion. Food makers' goal will be to convince their target to try their new recipes or continue with old ones; studios can advertise their latest blockbuster films directly onto them.

No matter what product they sell, their main objective is to increase sales; hence their attempts at persuasion. While they don't consider how this will impact you directly, so they must use subtle persuasion techniques so as not to alert or upset potential customers. As there may also be multiple brands trying to persuade you, each must find its own way of convincing their viewers of its perspective.

Due to the far-reaching effect of persuasion, its techniques have long been studied since ancient times. Influence is an invaluable asset that can be leveraged by anyone across many different circumstances and cultures.

Beginning in the early 20th century, formal studies of persuasion techniques began to gain ground. Remember that persuasion involves pushing an argument forward that convinces an audience and having them accept this message as their new way of living their lives.
Therefore, there is an immense need to discover effective persuasion techniques.

There are three dark persuasion techniques which have proven their worth over time and we will discuss these in this section.
Create a Need
One effective strategy for persuading someone to change their viewpoint or way of life is creating or capitalizing on a need that already exists for that individual, preferably done so in such a way as to be appealing and desirable by them. If done effectively and appropriately this tactic could yield great success with their intended target.

Persuaders must address what matters most to their target audience in order to succeed at persuasion - such as fulfilling dreams or increasing self-esteem - or providing shelter, love or food.

This approach always works well as it assumes that any subject requires some kind of help in some form or another - in other words, there is no one in need who doesn't dream and aspire for something in life - the persuader simply needs to find ways that they can assist the victim achieve these dreams more quickly and efficiently.

Persuaders often convince their target that making certain adjustments to their beliefs or perspective will help them realize their dreams faster, increasing the probability of success.

Example: A young man looking for intimate relations may promise a woman that he will help her improve her grades and finally make their parents proud by getting an A, but only if she becomes his friend. While this lady may believe that this young man truly cares about how well she performs academically, in reality he may only care about getting closer and engaging her sexually - academics being just an excuse for more sexual encounters!

Appeal to Social Needs

Persuaders may use another tactic for persuasion: identifying their target's social needs. While this technique may not bring immediate results, it still remains an invaluable asset in their toolbox.

People with an affinity for crowds and seeking attention tend to gravitate toward them naturally, seeking acceptance by joining in groups or having specific items as status symbols that give them the feeling that they belong in a higher class.

By appealing to their social needs, many TV commercials achieve success at appealing to viewers' purchasing decisions so that they won't "miss out." When advertisers can identify and appeal to specific social needs of a target, it can open up new areas of interest for that particular persona.

Words and Images Used as Loaded Signals

When persuading someone, words matter a lot and must be chosen carefully as each can have different impacts. There may be many ways of saying the same thing but one approach could prove more powerful than another.

Persuasion requires knowing when and how to say the right words at the right times; words are always key tools of communication and knowing the appropriate call-to-action words is paramount for successful persuasion.

Dark persuasion is one of the most potent tools of dark psychology, yet is often underestimated and neglected. Perhaps this is due to persuasion being unique as an attempt at mind control; unlike its alternatives that force submission on an unwilling target without their participation; unlike persuasion however, target decisions remain open with only limited interference from them at times being isolated to influence outcomes of process.

Persuasion works best when all cards are laid bare (albeit with hidden intentions in dark persuasion) so that its target can make the decision that best serves their interests.

Whilst brainwashing may refer to changing the thoughts and beliefs of others against their will or without their consent, its real definition is more expansive; it involves any systematic attempt at coercion and persuasion used to alter an individual's attitudes or alter their behaviors in order to alter behavior patterns and change behavioral outcomes.

Brainwashing tactics have long been employed as part of political indoctrination programs to get people to change their beliefs about politics or religious doctrines, particularly within cultic groups. Primarily, brainwashing works by replacing victim beliefs with those preferred by their captor and appropriate for the environment in which they exist.

Brainwashing involves stripping an individual of all freedom, independence and decision-making power; disrupting one's daily habits and behavior in such a way as to require complete obedience to authority of his/her captor in every aspect. Brainwashing often includes physical abuse as well as threats of injuries or death if necessary or life imprisonment before instilling new beliefs as an acceptable means for an enlightened life.

Brainwashing techniques aim to cultivate childlike trust between victim and captor, with victims encouraged to confess past crimes or make absurd or trivial errors for fear of appearing guilty before others have even had time to become brainwashed themselves. If other captors have also been brainwashed before them, these individuals could help reinforce this process by criticizing and showing displeasure with what the victim has done or failing to do in front of other members of society. Once brainwashing takes hold, captors begin receiving approvals and rewards for their acts. WATCH THIS VIDEO FOR HOW BRAINWASHING Can Be Part Of Dark Psychology

Dark psychology occurs when someone employs brainwashing tactics to influence another against their will and manipulate or influence them against their will. We each possess free will, meaning we should make our own decisions, associate freely, and choose who we associate with freely; when this freedom is taken away through force or coercion it constitutes dark psychology.

People in abusive relationships are susceptible to brainwashing. A husband might forbid his wife from socializing with certain friends on the pretext they will be detrimental influences - while she should make her own decision about this matter as she matures. Or worse, force their partner not wear certain types of clothing claiming it's unappealing so they can control them better.

Living with an abusive partner is both confusing and exhausting, often making life more complicated for everyone involved. They will blame and manipulate you for things that were never your responsibility; to keep their satisfaction you may become estranged from family and friends, change how you dress or your political views; it all becomes about them versus you.

An abusive relationship occurs when one partner uses brainwashing tactics to manipulate and control their partner. As a result, they become dependent upon them for simple decisions like selecting dinner. Their lives revolve solely around making their partner happy at any cost to themselves; and what constitutes love or how it should be expressed is determined solely by them - who then decides what exactly should make up happiness at their expense and vice versa. Their abuser is then responsible for defining love as expressed through them as well as anything wrong in the victim's life - from what needs improvement they should make or even how they should act accordingly and what constitutes appropriate behaviors in accordance with what their abusive partner defines what love should be expressed and defining everything about that victim's life so much like one-and what exactly that abuser wants them as regards behavior according to how one should conduct themselves and what behaviors would constitute appropriateness of what exactly this relationship.

Abuse comes in many forms; most frequently through emotional, psychological and physical abuse. Once inside their grasp, victims often cannot escape it.
An abusive partner soon finds ways to put down their partner with degrading remarks and insults, in order to maintain brainwashing and abuse. For their own psychological survival, there will occasionally be periods where their abuser will stop and show kindness towards their victim - creating trauma binds that make the victim want to make his or her abuser happy so as to be treated with warmth and kindness in return.

Brainwashing falls within dark psychology as its victim becomes trapped within their own life. A controlling partner in a relationship may withhold resources such as cars, money or food from their partner - turning him or her into a prisoner within their home, inducing fear in them and altering how they perceive the world around them.

Brainwashed victims' lives become consumed with thoughts of pleasing their abuser, even without physical violence being committed against them. Even without physical abuse occurring, their lives continue under the shadow of their abuser's presence; as a result, psychological effects such as anxiety disorders and depression often emerge as symptoms.

Brainwashing Process in Brief

Brainwashing is a systematic approach aimed at stripping one of their identity, altering beliefs, attitudes and values while also altering thought processes. Manipulators utilize various steps or stages as tools of brainwashing their victims.

Guilt
In a relationship, manipulators will constantly pick arguments in which their victims appear as the wrongdoers, making them feel guilty for every disagreement and leading them to feel shame for everything - this is the first stage in brainwashing a person.

Self-Betrayal
Being forced to denounce family and friends destroys one's sense of self while increasing guilt feelings; these sensations serve to break free of their past while creating space for creating a new identity.

Breaking Point
When victims of physical, verbal, and psychological assaults feel they've betrayed themselves and are made to feel guilty, they can reach the breaking point and collapse emotionally and psychologically. Crying uncontrollably and suffering anxiety attacks may be signs that something has broken loose within them; psychologically they fear they are losing themselves altogether and living in constant fear of losing themselves altogether.

Just when a victim feels powerless over themselves, an oppressor offers kindness as a respite from the assault on who they are. At such moments of light emerging where there was darkness, victims feel profound gratitude toward their attackers - an intentional move by their abusers before starting again on them.
At a time when victims are thankful to their abuser for helping them get to safety, the harsher side of his/her treatment often seems greater. They may feel they owe something back and feel obliged to repay his kindness - often by confessing their perceived mistakes to ease any guilt they might feel.

Channeling Guilt
Any feelings of guilt and shame the victim experiences will likely become complicated by an increased assault to their identity, leaving them uncertain what actions or decisions led them to believe they have committed and believing instead they must bear responsibility. As soon as the abuser perceives that guilt exists in them they use it for themselves, typically by convincing the victim they have led a life filled with bad decisions and ideologies; suggesting instead they open themselves up to new perspectives in order to change.

Logical Dishonoring A victim often believes their guilt lies with ideologies imposed externally; teachers and ideologies become the target for blame instead of seeing any manipulation at play. Confessions become one way of relieving guilt as the individual mentally discards any acts done under these "wrong" ideologies - thus symbolically distancing themselves from them and in doing so discrediting these perceptions of wrong ideology altogether.

Progress and Harmony
Rejecting old ideologies creates an opportunity for progress and harmony to emerge, since those opposed to it must now seek alternative views to replace it. If these appear compatible and suitable to their needs, the process speeds up significantly - providing peace in its place. At this point, calmness prevails, replacing any discomfort.
As punishment, those captured have suddenly been treated like heroes and kindhearted individuals are accepted as substitutes to replace sinful ideas in their old ideology.

Final Admittance and Rebirth

As soon as they encountered the stark contrast between past pain and future promise presented by their new ideology, the victim completely abandoned any allegiance to the old ideology by disclosing any remaining secrets; at that moment they took up full ownership of their new ideology.

Rebirth refers to this process and, depending on one's ideology, may include rites of passage that completely seal one into their new order. These may involve strong statements being spoken aloud for acceptance of new ideologies and swearing allegiance to new leaders.
Brainwashing: Exploring its Impact

Brainwashing, as previously explained, involves changing a person's thought patterns, beliefs and attitudes in order to control their behavior and gain control over them. This practice often occurs for the benefit of manipulators but can have devastating repercussions; there are various forms of impact brainwashing can have such as:

Brainwashing has a devastating impact on a victim's self-esteem. They feel they don't measure up and that nothing they do is good enough, leading them down a path of suicide or depression.

Anxiety Disorders - Someone being brainwashed often loses their sense of identity and becomes isolated from those closest to them. Forced to change from who they were previously, victims become constantly anxious not to do the wrong thing and may develop anxiety disorders which impact outward behaviors.

Depression - Brainwashed victims tend to become isolated from loved ones and the wider world, their focus being solely on pleasing their captor and receiving any kindness they offer in return. With no one to speak to and their feelings ignored by everyone around them, depression may set in, hindering relationships with others.

Lack of Self-Esteem - Constant abuse by their captor and criticism is enough to cause their victim to believe they have no worth and fear making any decisions because they have been taught they are unworthy.

Living in Fear - Brainwashers use fear tactics to influence their victims, making them fearful that something bad is waiting around the corner and that life in general is unsafe and unfriendly. Their victim lives with this constant worry that every person could pose danger if they venture outside, while captors use threats of consequences against their victim if he or she doesn't do what's required by their captor.
Change of Beliefs - the captor's primary goal is to shape their victims' beliefs so as to control their behavior and keep them under their thumb. No matter whether their belief was ethical; as long as it clashed with his or her ideologies or beliefs, then it wasn't good enough.

Dependent upon the intent of their captor or aggressor, brainwashing has different impacts on victims depending on its application. Therefore, it is vital to identify any techniques and tricks being employed by potential offenders to avoid falling prey to brainwashing techniques used by Dark Psychology practitioners. Below are a few such techniques commonly seen when engaging in Dark Psychology sessions.

Brainwashing occurs when individuals or groups use underhanded tactics to influence and persuade others against their will into changing their beliefs without their consent, often using psychological techniques such as dark psychology. Influencing and persuasion techniques used against their will are also known as brainwashing tactics, as it involves underhand tactics used by an individual or group in an attempt to brainwash another. While people experience persuasion every day, when this becomes forced change without consent it becomes brainwashing and dark psychology tactics begin being employed against them this can include any number of tactics employed against their victims by different parties that include:

Isolation - the initial step of brainwashing usually entails isolating their victim from family and friends. By isolating them completely from society, the manipulator wants their victim to have no one they can talk to about their manipulation tactics; otherwise their authority would be challenged by third parties, giving their opponent more information from various sources than themselves.

Attack of Self-Esteem - When victims are isolated, manipulators find it easier to break them down and build them back up again in accordance with his desires. For successful brainwashing to occur, however, victims must first feel inferior to the manipulator and this often involves ridicule, intimidation or mocking by the latter which further diminishes self-esteem of victims who feel they're completely vulnerable before becoming victims themselves.

Mental Abuse - Manipulators often employ psychological torture in order to brainwash their victims, such as telling lies about them in front of others to make them look foolish, as well as badgering or depriving their victims of any personal space so that they feel trapped by them.

Physical abuse - Manipulators use various physical methods to subjugate their victims and influence them, including depriving them of food or access to water sources. Manipulators often rob their victims of sleep by employing violence against them, depriving them of food, and keeping the room cold. A manipulator may also employ subtle ways of brainwashing their victims; such as keeping noise levels elevated, having constantly flickering lights or deliberately altering room temperatures.

Repetitive Music - According to studies, playing repetitive beats can induce a hypnotic state in people. A manipulator who understands this technique can use this tactic against their victim. The rhythm of music can alter consciousness until their manipulator can use this tactic and speak directly into your subconscious - thus leading your brain to respond immediately with new suggestions, thus changing behavior automatically.

Contact is only permitted with other brainwashed individuals - The manipulator only permits their victim to have contact with other victims of his/her manipulative campaign, hoping for peer pressure from other victims to persuade their target into submission of his or her new way of thinking. Feeling lonely and isolated, victims tend to heed suggestions made by others so as to feel accepted and feel less alone.

Us vs Them - When manipulators introduce an Us and Them dynamic, it seems as if they are giving their victim a choice between themselves and perceived enemies; all in an attempt to gain complete obedience from them. Having shown the negative aspects of others, manipulators expects their victim to select themselves over them as opposed to choosing others over themselves.

Love Bombing - With this tactic, the manipulator draws their victim closer by showing physical affection through touching, exchanging intimate thoughts, bonding emotionally and showing kindness - this tactic is used to show validation to their victim that joining their group was the right decision, erasing any affection they might feel towards anyone outside.

Brainwashing rarely serves the greater good. Most manipulators employ such tactics in order to gain full and total control of their victims.
Brainwashing can be devastating to its victims. They quickly lose any sense of themselves and live to please their captor; simple things we take for granted such as choosing what and when to wear are taken from them; any decisions they might otherwise be making are taken away from them - all this so the manipulator feels unworthy and grateful that they've won their favour.

Step one in avoiding brainwashing is becoming aware of the tactics manipulators use and their traits, so as to recognize when someone tries to brainwash you or someone close. Brainwashing is an aggressive form of dark psychology wherein a manipulator uses these tactics for personal gain while disregarding their victims' feelings or wellbeing.

Now that you understand all of the ways others have caused harm to yourself, it's time to harness this knowledge and use it for good. No matter what you thought in the past about your brain and abilities, you now realize you possess incredible power that was given to you at birth - capabilities which may or may not be readily used. Some may struggle to come to grips with who they truly are and their goals in life, and that's perfectly okay; trying too hard can limit our thinking and prevent new insights from appearing. No matter how others have made you feel in the past, their actions do not define who you are today. Take lessons from your history while remaining true to who and where you came from. Let go of any hurt you have felt so you can begin healing and moving in a more positive direction.

Make sure that you spend enough time getting to know people well, without making assumptions about them. The more that you understand who people truly are at their core, the easier it will be for you to have a positive influence over them. Even when feeling lost and confused, digging inward or externally might reveal more meaningful truths; when making assumptions or labelling people too quickly will only limit your capacity for growth and understanding the world better.

Communication will be key. While it might be scary and challenging, speaking the truth out will eventually be beneficial in finding solutions to problems more efficiently.
At the end of the day, speaking out and sharing your truth will make you feel much better - both yourself and others will benefit from hearing what's on your mind and heart. Don't try to persuade other ways besides communicating. Don't withhold anything from anyone who may need something; manipulating others this way won't get anywhere close to achieving lasting change compared to talking things out through dialogue and talking it all through with another individual.

Now is the time to put all the pain you have experienced to good use. Everything has led up to where you are today, the darkest moments which seemed unending have passed, and all those times when you wanted nothing but escape brought you where you are today. Though you may never want to repeat these experiences again, learn to be thankful for them as without them, your future would likely look very different and less beneficial for others.
Now is the time to do what you probably desire most of all - influence others! In today's society, persuasion is key and failing to persuade certain individuals can keep you from realizing the things you truly desire in this lifetime. Therefore, getting to

know who it is you want to convince is of paramount importance - whether that be convincing your husband you're ready for children, or convincing an entire 100-member sales team of the importance of pushing harder to drive sales; understanding them begins by getting acquainted with who they are and their operating style before approaching them directly and trying them personally!

At this stage, it's essential to first gain an understanding of their background: age, gender identity and location are just a few questions to keep an eye out for when building persuasion strategies that fit your interests. By answering such queries accurately, forming strategies of persuasion becomes much simpler.

Certain differences will play an essential role in this situation. For example, approaching your 18-year-old boyfriend for $20 differs considerably from asking your 80-year-old grandmother the same thing. To effectively persuade people, it is crucial that you understand both what generically characterize them and their unique individual characteristics such as those which make up their personality traits.

Once you understand their interests and what makes them happy, the next step should be assessing what would encourage sales if necessary - such as discounts, freebies or other rewards for being customers.
Once you understand their likes and dislikes, the next step should be identifying those things they dislike - such as long return times after purchasing something, hidden fees or not being able to customize their products. Once identified, acting accordingly becomes simple; whenever something offends them provide something they like as a solution; although this seems obvious many who attempt to influence other will overlook this step.

Finally, ensure you are mindful of how others communicate. By understanding this dynamic, it will become much simpler to ensure you express things the same way with them. Always listen to what the other person is saying and provide them a platform to speak. Pay attention not just to what words they're using but their face as they share information with you. If someone feels they are being ignored they could turn away and far less likely be persuaded in the long run - the next section will explore this subject further and how best you can foster healthy interactions in life.
Understanding Communication Fundamentals

Communication can be challenging for all of us. At first glance it may appear effortless - just open your mouth and start talking - but many find themselves struggling to express how they're feeling in words alone, even though they might experience it themselves. But the more effective communication becomes in life the easier life will become and happier the resultant outcomes will be.

To improve your communication skills, remember that improving them requires practice. There's no magic pill or secret way of improving instantly - in order to become better, you must continually interact with other people through conversations - whether with baristas in coffee shops or strangers at bus stops, starting small conversations is best when starting off - don't bother other people though, just look for ways in which you can articulate your voice beyond saying the standard "how are you?."

Make sure that you are effectively communicating your feelings to yourself. Even when we are alone, sometimes our emotions still don't make complete sense to us. If necessary, start journaling daily your emotions; the more that you can work them out on your own through writing down emotions that arise, the easier it will be to manage them on your own and share them effectively with others.

When starting to persuade others, be wary of your words. Don't force anyone into doing anything or put them in situations in which they feel powerless to stop themselves - avoid phrases such as "You should do this." No one likes being told what to do!
Speaking first about yourself may seem counterintuitive, but people will respond more positively by picking up on examples rather than hearing you dictate their behavior directly. For instance, let's say you want to persuade your spouse to start getting up earlier so as to reduce stress due to being late every morning; rather than saying something like, "You should wake up earlier," you could instead say: "By starting earlier I have found that by being less stressed during morning commute time by getting up earlier it has greatly decreased stress levels for myself and helped reduce my morning stressor before work!"

Letting others believe your idea is theirs will ensure greater credibility of persuasion; people like to feel they came up with it themselves rather than being forced into accepting something against their will. Allow them to work through it on their own so they can assess its benefits and drawbacks themselves - this way you will create more effective persuasion rather than forcing something onto them.

After this, take special care with both your tone and body language, creating an environment where they feel at ease when around you. Showing kindness, love and compassion will allow them to relate better with you; don't feel pressured into rigid and harsh communication strategies just so people will do what you want - instead try being kind and gentle instead and they will respond better!

At last, make sure that you treat those you are trying to influence with respect. Don't make them feel ashamed or embarrassed around you if they say something silly; build them up instead and they will reciprocate this kind of kindness in return.
How to Convert Negative Manipulation Into Positive Persuasion

Now you should be an expert on basic level psychology! Everything starts in our mind and manifests differently for every individual. In order to truly achieve what you desire in this life, it's crucial that you begin learning about other people and how their brain works; otherwise you risk suffering irreparable damage in due time.

Take all of the manipulative techniques that you have learned in the past and use it now for good. Learn from your negative experiences so you can use them as learning experiences on how not to treat others. In order to transition negative manipulation into positive persuasion, start by having good intentions behind what you want others to agree to - something mutually beneficial between both parties should be the end goal of any negotiation between both of you. Listen carefully when speaking with other individuals as to their needs so you can reach an agreement where both can get positive benefits in return from both parties involved - this way both parties win in terms of positive benefits at once!

Make sure that you prioritize meeting the needs of others over your own. Of course, taking care of yourself first is important, but being unaware of how others feel won't serve anyone well in the long run.

Influencers are leaders. If you have good ideas that you wish to impart to other people and wish for them to gain from what you know, it is imperative that you develop and hone positive leadership abilities.

Others should not be seen as tools of yours alone. Others can help, but you must help them as well. A great leader knows how to motivate others without forcing their will; in other words, providing something beneficial in return. While you might find someone willing to assist with reaching your dreams, be wary that doing so comes at no cost or benefit to themselves or you.
Your beliefs must also be part of this journey if you wish to achieve anything significant in life. Align yourself and center them around this system, and your success is certain!

Be sure to use an inclusive language when speaking to others, using "we" language and confidence when doing so. They will likely pay more attention when included as part of this process themselves.

At this stage of your development, the key component is having a growth mindset. Limiting our thoughts leads to us realizing less potential in life, so keep up-to-date with studies related to persuasion, manipulation and psychology in general as well as subscribing to newsletters or magazines about the human brain in order to gain a deeper insight into its workings.

Check in regularly with your health. Failing to care for all aspects of yourself could seriously compromise the functioning of your mind as we get older, so now is the time to ensure we prepare our minds accordingly. Practice keeping an open perspective and listening closely when communicating with others; continue learning because the more knowledge you gather the more there will still be to discover.

Never use aggression and persuasion either. While fear may work to get people to do what you want temporarily, long-term respect should never be gained through fearful methods alone. Show your compassion and understand others more fully so they will listen more attentively when sharing what is on their minds.

When analyzing another person, body language is key. Are they tall or do they slump over? Observing someone's eyes, face, and arms can reveal much about who they truly are - for instance you could notice that someone who seems confident may actually be suffering from anxiety if you start paying attention. You could also discover someone you trusted was lying to you!

Finding out what distinguishes someone from others and understanding why they act a certain way can be tricky, but you will eventually start to gain more of an insight into why someone behaves this way. Although no two people will ever fully be understood, you can at least start to gain a glimpse into why some act the way they do.

Once you can successfully analyze someone, the next step should be convincing them of your viewpoints or demands. Persuasion is key when trying to get what you want from life or at least deserve from others; just as we discussed in book one, reading will do nothing without action being taken - although becoming aware of yourself may be daunting at first, this step is essential towards becoming aware of others around you and becoming effective communicators.

People often follow others blindly without ever going deeper within themselves and challenging their thoughts and making an honest effort to do this. While this may be challenging at first glance, it's crucial that we explore our psyche in order to live happier and healthier lives.

Remind yourself that it's still healthy and normal to allow others to influence you! Think about all the great leaders around the world who may have inspired others by inspiring positive passion and motivation within those they lead - many have done exactly this with you in mind!
No one is to blame if they succumb to the influence of others; what will make a difference now is whether that influence comes in the form of positive and uplifting inspiration rather than manipulation from someone who seeks to harm you.

As you navigate life, keep this in mind as a key goal: always use your brain for good! Although this might be challenging at times, doing so is always the better solution. Even when manipulated easily by another, don't take advantage of such opportunities to manipulate someone. While this might seem like their fault for not being more aware, never assume this; some individuals have experienced things which have made breaking free from old patterns more challenging and finding healthier solutions to cope with emotions and thoughts.

Always assist others, not harm them. Even those who may have wronged you in the past shouldn't become targets of your anger; use your intelligence for good, helping make the world a better place with healthy influence, and you will soon discover everything you have ever desired will come your way.

All Achieve Success Start with the Brain

An individual analyzer or reader can quickly decipher an individual's personality through various attributes, including what he or she does in their spare time. For example, participating in community drives, volunteering activities, and contributing to church initiatives could reveal they are philanthropic. On the other hand, partying endlessly or watching television could indicate low ambition and instant gratification; even seemingly trivial habits reveal much about who people really are.
How Psychology Impacts Our Lives

Psychologists disagree about whether our behavior is solely determined by genetics or heredity; others consider our experiences since birth to be key contributors. Others hold the belief that our immediate environment or experiences shape our behavior - for instance if someone experiences constant abuse then their behavior could change as a result. For instance if a person constantly undergoes abuse then their behaviors might change accordingly;
As they grow up and experience marginalization and racism due to their class or race, they may come to despise wealthier people or seemingly superior races while sympathizing with those oppressed.

Likewise, children who experience persistent bullying, abuse or victimization as children may grow up to be bullies themselves. Their outlook, values, personality and attitude will likely have been formed by such early experiences of violence and abuse in early life.

Have you come across people who seem intent on reading their personality through zodiac signs or astrology? Isn't this indicative of low self-awareness and understanding? For example, people tend to gravitate toward things they lack much of; someone deprived of adequate parental attention in early childhood or teen years might become someone who enjoys drama and attention-seeking strategies in adulthood, perhaps becoming increasingly dramatic and showy over time.

People analyzers should remain alert for subtle cues that may give away who the person really is. There are plenty of signs to be found around us; all you need to do as an analyst is keep an eye out.
mes

Our mind can be divided into three distinct layers - conscious mind, subconscious mind and unconscious mind. Whereas conscious awareness encompasses thoughts, actions, learnings and experiences from conscious awareness alone, subconscious and unconscious minds are realms within the mind that may contain information we don't realize is present; through conscious mind awareness we gain an awareness of all perceptions, feelings, concepts or ideas gathered from our immediate environment that might otherwise remain unseen or unknown to us.

However, when it comes to our subconscious and unconscious minds, we typically have very limited awareness of all of their thoughts, ideas, concepts, and information stored there. Our conscious mind only shows part of its complexity; there are multiple layers beneath its surface which affect our personality and behavior without our awareness.

Start with yourself if you want to become an effective people analyst. Assess how much you know or how well you understand yourself or your own personality or behavior patterns, including any triggers that drive your behaviors - what beliefs, fears, motivators or values could be driving such behavior?

Once you understand yourself and the various personalities and behaviors, begin exploring those of close friends and family members. After this step is completed, attempt to understand strangers such as those you see while waiting at doctor's clinics or airports as well as people you meet for the first time at parties or during everyday interactions - continue practicing this skill until it comes naturally and can read people quickly and effectively like an expert!

Emotions and Human Behavior

Emotions are fleeting experiences we have as part of mental activity. While emotions may seem rational or logical at first, sometimes our reactions remain emotional despite evidence against the friend being threatened or accused. For example, even when presented with evidence of wrongdoing on their part.
Even when someone betrays us behind our back, we remain loyal and trust them more.

As humans, we tend to act on impulse rather than reasoning. People's behaviors are heavily influenced by emotions. Understanding them gives us the power to understand and predict their actions, personality traits and behavioral patterns. Psychological Theories
Classical Conditioning is a widely-held psychological theory in which individuals learn by associating certain behaviors with rewards or reinforcers, such as treats. The same principle is often employed when training animals - for instance when rewarding your dog with treats every time he retrieves a ball! Inevitably, fetching will become

associated with treats for your pet; eventually it learns that fetching is necessary if he wants a treat!

Classical conditioning plays a large part in our lives as humans. From birth, we associate crying with being fed and kept clean; to studying consistently to earn good grades in school. Classical conditioning influences every aspect of life - babies learn that crying means they will get fed or cleaned; students discover studying diligently results in good grades. Therefore, classical conditioning remains influential throughout life: as individuals we learn how to respond to certain stimuli in certain ways - making up one of the key determinants when it comes to behavior analysis.

Human Behavior and Physiology.

Studies show that people exhibit specific physical reactions to stimuli which can be used as indicators when it comes to analyzing them. Criminal psychologists commonly utilize this principle in understanding criminal psychology and what motivates criminals to commit crimes; with biometric technology investigators attempt to ascertain if suspect thoughts align with actions.

Psychological and physiological techniques combined are powerful tools for uncovering the motivations for human behavior. Our bodies exhibit specific physiological reactions when someone engages in deception or lies, such as dilated pupils, perspiration or other indicators that they might be misleading or lying. Heart rate increases, palpitations increases, sweating increases and toe twitching occur more often when feeling threatened or uncomfortable. Analyzing people using physiological or nonverbal clues may provide more accurate analysis; however, like with all forms of analysis it cannot ever be 100% reliable.

However, not all forms of communication have the ability to persuade people, as some may simply serve to entertain or provide information. Persuasion can also be used as an unsavory means to manipulate others; trying to persuade others may even be considered repulsive behavior. Persuasion should be distinguished from communication as its cause is given rise to changes in behavioral changes as an effect or response.

Here, we will explore the stages a person goes through when being persuaded. First is communication wherein receiver pays attention to content provided. He or she will then attempt to comprehend all aspects of the communication as a whole, including trying to comprehend what the speaker is trying to convey. This includes understanding what conclusions the speaker is proposing as well as any evidence which may support this conclusion. Persuasion occurs when an individual accepts or agrees with what is being provided and retains that interest long enough to act upon it. The primary goal of persuasion is for an individual or a group of people to adopt new attitudes, such as switching brands of cereal due to new information presented or altering religious beliefs.

Conditioning Theories Conditioning is one of the primary concepts in persuasion. Conditioning seeks to convince someone of something on their own rather than giving direct instructions such as obedience.

Conditioning is widely employed by advertisers in advertising to generate positive associations between their brand or logo and positive emotions. Companies resort to commercials that encourage viewers to laugh, feel sentimental or use happy music and images; once these commercials conclude they reveal the brand logo with hopes that these emotions connect with their product or service.

Inoculation Theory The inoculation theory can often be observed in comparative advertisements. According to this concept, one side has weak arguments that may cause their credibility to be reduced and thus make their audience choose another party's superior arguments instead.

Narrating Transportation Theory.

The narrative transportation theory postulates that attitudes of people can change when they immerse themselves in stories. It seeks to demonstrate the persuasive power of stories by explaining when individuals might experience narrative transportation due to meeting various preconditions; furthermore, narrative transportation occurs when listening to narratives which invoke certain feelings such as empathy for its characters.

Extract From:"How To Analyze People and Body Language For Beginners. Gaining Insight Into Body And Brain Secrets To Gain Extraordinary Communication Skills Mindset NLP."

THE END